JOB BE DAMNED

Rishi Piparaiya spent over fifteen years as a flunky, middle manager and senior executive in multinational corporations. He ran international strategy projects out of Citigroup's New York headquarters, built risk management models for Banco Santander in Spain, launched innovative products and services for Citi India, and led a national sales force and award-winning marketing team for Aviva.

He did make concerted efforts to scuttle his career by regularly sending satirical memos at work and boycotting all meetings that started before 10 a.m. But he still stumbled up the corporate ladder, with designations such as AVP, VP, SVP and CXO before realizing that there must be more to life than accumulating letters of the alphabet. So he safely evacuated from his C-suite office to a journey where he does what he likes, whether mentoring entrepreneurs in makeshift offices or envisioning future books on blank pages.

A dusty briefcase in his Mumbai home holds certificates from Cornell University, the University of Rochester, the University of Cambridge and the Cathedral & John Connon School.

His first book *Aisle Be Damned* is a national bestseller.

Praise for *Job Be Damned*

'I had a hearty laugh as I read this incisive take on everyday corporate life. A very well written work from a very humorous and talented professional.' – **P.S. Jayakumar**, Managing Director and CEO, Bank of Baroda

'A hilarious Masters in Bullshit Administration for the inveterate corporate ladder climber, that flows straight from the gut. With his extensive experience around professional dung slingers, Rishi provides uproarious tips and tricks in his distinctive sardonic style, for navigating the corporate kerfuffle, lovingly called a career.' – **Gourav Rakshit**, President and CEO, Shaadi.com

'There is the trade and then, Rishi's book offers 250+ pages of tricks of the trade. From hacking town hall meetings to your advantage, to such horrors of corporate life as the conference call, *Job Be Damned* is the de rigueur management book you truly need. Move over Drucker, this is Everything You Seriously Needed To Know About Corporate Life, But Didn't Know Whom To Ask.' – **Rayomand J. Patell,** Executive Creative Director, Havas India

'Rishi lances the boil on the rear of the corporate world with wit and an ironic voice. *Job Be Damned* is a damn good primer to bamboozle your colleagues, get ahead and be king rat in the corporate rat race!' – **Ajai Jhala**, CEO, BBDO India

'As an entrepreneur and former corporate executive, I was cracking up at every step. I could see, VERY vividly, situations and conversations that I've been a part of at some point or the other, over the past two decades. The writing just flows - rich with clever analogies and a lightness of tone, albeit ripe with sarcasm. Superb!' – **Romil Ratra**, CEO, The A, Apex Clubs

JOB
BE
DAMNED

Work less. Career Success.

RISHI
PIPARAIYA

HarperCollins *Publishers* India

First published in India by
HarperCollins *Publishers* in 2018
A-75, Sector 57, Noida, Uttar Pradesh 201301, India
www.harpercollins.co.in

2 4 6 8 10 9 7 5 3 1

P-ISBN: 978-93-5277-767-9
E-ISBN: 978-93-5277-768-6

Typeset in 10.5/14.1 PT Serif at
Manipal Digital Systems, Manipal

Printed and bound at
Thomson Press (India) Ltd

This is for you, Dad

Dear Ankur & Poorvi,

Hope you enjoy this!
To finding true calling!

Best,
Rishi

CONTENTS

AUTHOR'S NOTE

You are an exceptional professional; something tells me that you are. The sharpest knife in the organizational toolbox, you are smarter than others and much more hardworking. The strongest rung of the corporate ladder, you are conscientious and focus on business priorities. As the fizziest can in the company canteen, you care deeply about self-development, which explains your intent stare at this wordy page in an age of listicles, slideshows and thirty-second videos.

But something's not quite right. Despite all your skills and capabilities, you somehow seem to be trailing behind all the losers around you. You painstakingly did all the hard work, but your boss swooped in and took the credit. No one deserved that promotion more than you, but the politician in the next cubicle somehow swung it in his favour. You were about to get that coveted posting, but it was mercilessly snatched away purely because of bad luck. However, you still maintain your faith that the universe recognizes your potential and it's only a matter of time before your organization acknowledges your talent.

Let me step in here with my sharp stylus and burst your bubble: **It's not going to happen.** You are, what I term, an **amateur professional**. You are merely one amongst hundreds of millions of people, festering in a corporate world that is filled with average professionals. Take a walk around your office, peer into all the cubicles and observe those robots, mindlessly staring at computer screens oblivious to your presence. Grab a morning coffee, stand at any bus stop, taxi stand or train station and witness the suited rats scurrying with their laptop bags. Look everywhere around you—everyone is average. Average professionals in average jobs with average companies in average industries doing average work for average pay leading to average bonuses that will be spent on average holidays. And by swimming in the same salty sea of mediocrity, you are automatically average as well.

In the true spirit of capitalism, self-styled management gurus, theoretical business school professors and inept consultants have sprung up to exploit your delusions. They state that you are inherently exceptional but simply need to refocus your brilliance by following some suspect success principles. You read their books to learn the habits of extremely effective people, how to make friends and sway people, how to destroy all the rules, survive the first ninety days, wear a bunch of thinking hats, work few-hour workweeks and become a single minute manager. You try to understand how corporations are re-engineered, how companies go from good to great, are built to last, how blue ocean strategies are developed, how to compete for the future and cross the chasm. You marvel at case studies and biographies of high achievers and convince yourself that you are also just one good idea away from fame and fortune.

And you keep the faith that one day you will make a difference.

But millions of people are absorbing that hogwash and still running in circles. Despite all the reading that is done globally, the top ten individuals have more wealth than the bottom half of the world's population. The Fortune 500 companies employ over twenty-five million people, but only 500 make it as CEOs. And that stack of books in your library notwithstanding, you still report to a dunderhead of a boss, whose idea of compelling non-fiction is his daily horoscope.

Reading all that gobbledygook will get you nowhere. On the other hand, *Job Be Damned* is just the page-turner to turn the page on your career. It recognizes that the path to excellence is crowded, imaginary and pointless. Its goal is far more achievable—it appreciates that you are amongst average people and focuses on making you the best average professional that you can be. There is no 'aim for the moon, and you'll at least land among the stars' bullshit happening here—we are aiming squarely for the treetop, and we will get there. And we will do this without any management jargon or mumbo-jumbo—just practical instruction on how to sparkle through the indefinite dull existence that all professionals live through.

Starting from exaggerating your CV, fluffing your interview, elbowing through group discussions, lowballing performance expectations and brown-nosing your boss, we will ensure that the foundations of your career are rock solid. Work is a perpetual cycle of attending meetings, procrastinating and covering your ass, and by the end of this section, you will master this holy trinity. We will then work on the critical corporate skills of making confusing conversation, writing befuddling emails, delivering perplexing presentations and navigating the toughest of business reviews. Your perception is the most important thing that you will manage in your career, and we will develop strategies to make you look awesome, your colleagues seem bad, and everything else appear opaque.

By now, you will have a renewed energy towards your spectacularly unexciting job, and we will navigate the innocuous pitfalls that befall most people—birthday celebrations, off-sites, group photographs, town halls and other career minefields. Next, senior leaders will learn how to manipulate employees, employees will learn how to manipulate appraisals, and aspiring consultants will learn how to manipulate everyone. Finally, we'll understand how you can maximize the unlikely event of transitioning to a better job or the more probable eventuality of getting unceremoniously sacked.

Whether you are an apprehensive fresher considering your first job, a valiant middle manager staving off the wolves around you or a burned out senior leader who wakes up each morning wishing that he were doing anything else, you will find relevance in this book. Because all this while you have been receiving mediocre advice on how to be really good, but for the first time here's practical wisdom on how to be really good at being mediocre. This is what **professional professionals** like your bosses and colleagues have known and implemented all along. And now you can also be a member of the corporate illuminati.

Happy reading and may your job be damned.

HOW TO USE THIS BOOK

Starting from the job search and ending at one's invariable termination, I have attempted to cover all the important aspects of corporate life that a typical professional might encounter. The ideas in this book, while written primarily in the backdrop of large multinational work environments, are fairly universal and applicable to all kinds of organizations.

Some of the notions only apply to some employees, depending on their career stage. These sections have been identified, basis the group of employees they are most relevant to, with the below icons.

Early Careers   Middle Management   Senior Leadership

I have occasionally included real-world examples of other average companies, professionals and events so that you can revel in the mediocrity of others. Titled 'Feel Good Anecdotes', I hope you'll find the failures of others motivating.

For the sake of my writing convenience, I have primarily used the masculine gender, however 'him' and 'her' can be interchangeably applied virtually throughout the book. Finally, as you will very quickly observe, I have an inherent tendency to generalize. You will get used to it.

THE DIS-ORGANIZATION

People work simply because they have nothing better to do. If they had a superior way of using their time, they would not waste it on something that, to start with, is called 'work'. And if work were indeed fun, people would be clamouring to do it, moreover for free. But that's rarely the case, and so all these folk reluctantly find their way into organizations, which are nothing but groups of boring people who all hate each other. To impart an artificial sense of unity, organizations give them a name—employees, from the Middle French term, employé—an individual who provides labour to a company or another person. This does sound a lot more politically correct than slave, from the Old French term, *esclave*—someone who is bound to the land and owned by the feudal lord.

Organizations then ask their employees to pursue a common goal, which they term a 'mission'. And while it is camouflaged with ample flowery prose, all mission statements are effectively the same.

> We aim to make pots of money for our senior leadership by gracefully ripping off our customers and selling as much as we can of our products and services at a price higher than what they are worth. We need people to achieve this, and we will try and treat them humanely … at least sometimes.

Now, most employees find it very difficult to appreciate, understand or deliver on this mission, so they come up with an easier goal to be accountable for—finding scapegoats. Significant time and effort is therefore invested in finding other employees to blame when things go wrong. It's an equally worthy cause.

Types of Organizations

Organizations range from young start-ups to large, established multinational corporations, and as you evaluate prospective hellholes to burn in, consider three important factors.

Cachet: A job provides a misguided sense of self-worth like nothing else can. To maximize the artificial boost to your self-esteem, assess how sexy your visiting card will look when you flash it to others. The company name, your designation and your prospective email ID are some of the key attributes that influence the organization's snob value.

Culture: In the world of science, bacteria are cultivated in an artificial medium that provides them nutrients—this is called culture. In the workplace, you are the bacteria, and the senior leaders are the mad scientists who are poking the pooch with pipettes—this is termed work culture. Carefully assess all the senior whackos at each laboratory that you are considering and especially their leader, the CEO. The work culture usually flows down from there.

Compensation: By taking on a job, you damage your mental facility and peace of mind, for which you are given a salary as compensation. Usually, even that is not sufficient for the trauma undergone and additional disbursements, called perks, are made. Add up all the inflows, compare it to the cost of selling your soul and then make your final decision.

Some kooks suggest that people should consider a fourth C – **Contentment** as they evaluate jobs. They hypothesize that enjoying work will lead to happiness, which should be the primary criterion for choosing one's vocation. If one loves what one does, the cachet is irrelevant, culture can be influenced, and compensation will follow. It's quite a laughable concept and not worth delving into as it will simply detract us from our march to mediocrity.

1. Start-Ups

Cachet Start-ups are typically formed when a group of college friends get plastered at a house party and come up with an idea for a website. They name the company by taking a common noun, changing a letter and then frantically checking if the dotcom domain of the word they have coined is available. For example, a Tomato could become Bomato, Flipcart can become Tripkart, Grocers can be Brocers. The person who slurred, 'Let's make a website,' is crowned CEO, the geek who builds a prototype over the weekend is anointed CTO, and the bartender is appointed COO.

The prestige of working at a start-up is cyclical—at some point it is a very cool place to be and soon after, one of the most pitiful jobs that you could work at. Time your entry carefully—as soon as you see executives from large organizations joining the start-up, know that the end is near.

Culture: The organizational culture mirrors the maturity of its young and reckless founders, and it's a breakneck journey with all important decisions made via coin toss. The founders eventually end up nabbing a few rounds of funding too many at which point they cede control to venture capitalists. External investors finally bring some method to this madness and replace the coin with a dartboard.

Compensation: Start-ups primarily pay in stock options, a mythical currency that consistently increases in theoretical value until everyone is a multimillionaire on paper. Then one day, poof! it disappears, and all are back to being worthless.

2. Small and Medium Enterprises (SMEs)

Cachet: Small and medium enterprises are the backbone of the economy and are usually involved in importing and exporting something, somewhere. They were typically founded by a far-sighted entrepreneur, who is now a photograph on the wall, and are presently managed by a gaggle of his descendants. The company name, therefore, boasts an assortment of names, surnames and relationships—Patel & Sons, Kothari Brothers, Kanga, Shah and Kotwal Partners and so on. Given the complexity of such names, your email ID will be on a Gmail server. If your surname features in the company name, even if you are unrelated to the founders, strongly consider working there; you will garner tremendous respect, purely by this coincidental association. If not, there is little acclaim you will get at sharing your 'Manager, Jignesh Mehta and First Cousins Pvt Ltd' visiting card with anyone.

Culture: All relatives sit in a small cabin, on medium size chairs that barely accommodate their large girths. They spend time juggling accounts, cooking books, jabbering on phones and domineering Gaurishankar the peon, who's on perpetual standby outside the communal cabin. As soon as any of their children reach puberty, they are indoctrinated into the business. And sooner or later, all of these uncles, aunties, nieces, nephews and cousins will clash, charring you in the crossfire.

Compensation: Your compensation, in the months that you get paid, is just about enough to keep you above the poverty line. Perks include luxuries like tap water and oxygen and a 2 per cent employee discount on whatever it is that Motabhai Mehta and his extended family of hucksters are peddling.

3. Public Sector Undertakings (PSUs)

Cachet: These organizational dinosaurs have been around since India's Independence and will still be plodding long after the corporate world has imploded. They invariably have India, Bharat, National or an Indian state in their name and their line of business is self-explanatory—National Garam Shakti Company, Bank of (insert Indian state), Desh Ki Oil Corporation, etc. Most PSUs are still developing their websites and configuring dial-up modems to access the internet, and you likely won't get an email ID. But fear not, a retinue of stationed office boys will deliver your memos and messages faster and more efficiently than any 4G data connection.

Culture: The general work culture is of 'picnics and procrastination'. It's a hierarchy driven structure with the chairman squatting at the top and the rest of the organization squarely focused on keeping him happy. When it comes to appointing the chairman, a rigid system of 'there shall be no logic followed' is followed. Numerous candidates are put through a triathlon across the vigilance departments, respective ministries and the prime minister's office, and the winners are randomly deployed to head various PSUs. For the next few years, it is the usual *veni, vidi, destroychi—I came, I oversaw, I destroyed*—routine.

Compensation: While the absolute salary is a rounding error for most people, when measured on per unit of work done, you'll give billionaires a run for their money. And even Gates and Bezos don't get perks like cars with beacon lights and unfettered access to Dak Bungalow guesthouses across the country. You need to pass just one common entrance exam, and you can spend the rest of your career in Luckingham Palace.

4. Multinational Companies (MNCs)

Cachet: MNCs started operations in one home market but have now spread their tentacles to scores of countries around the world. They have cool western names e.g. Onlylever, City, Sonny, and own their respective domains. These organizations are at the top of the status pyramid and in family weddings and gatherings, you will often overhear the proud phrase, 'My son/daughter is working with an American Yemen Sea.'

Culture: The work culture is professionally political. The CEO has the typical 'IIT-IIM-but I still got a second MBA abroad' educational combo. His fortunes are intricately linked to the global CEO who appointed him and when he gets sacked, so does our hero. This happens quite often, and with this kind of career volatility, the primary intent of most people is to protect their turf. Consequently, you will find that the perspectives and timeframes of most MNC employees are somewhat different from others. The short-term is now, the medium-term the coming week, and the long-term, for those who can even think that far ahead, is next month.

Compensation: There really is little to complain about. Your monthly salary hits your account with a precision that would make a Swiss watch envious, and a quantum that would make a Swiss bank blush. Moreover, you will make frequent foreign trips that will allow you awesome social media perks such as 'check-ins' at international airport lounges.

5. Indian Multinationals

Cachet: Indian multinationals either have a cool but meaningless name, e.g. Outfosys or Banraxy or are an acronym of humdrum words, e.g. ICICICICI (Indian Corporation and Investment Cupcakes and International Credit and Intelligent Calculations of India) or DTC (Desi Tambaku Company). They often improvise on their domain name e.g. www.dtcportal.com.

Culture: They are bang in the middle of the competitive circle, competing against every other type of corporation from start-ups to MNCs, and the work culture is extremely stressful. The CEO has usually been with the company since inception and is continually trying to balance his role as a patriarch and professional executive. If he ever passes on the baton, it's with trembling fingers to another piece of lumbering woodwork. The leadership team is a mishmash of internal old-timers and external executives and the culture, therefore, is usually in complete disarray.

Compensation: Though not as lucrative as MNCs, what you lose in cash and foreign selfies, is more than made up via stock options. And unlike the ones doled out by start-ups, these are usually worth a decent packet by the time you get sacked.

6. Family Conglomerates

Cachet: Family conglomerates were founded a few generations ago by a truly visionary patriarch, whose bust adorns the corporate office lobby. These behemoths are present in all lines of business, from paper to panties, and are headed by a member of the founding family, who is admiringly known as the 'lala'. These organizations are therefore also reverently referred to as 'lala companies'. Lala companies typically have the family surname as an integral part of their corporate name, but please do not place complete reliance on this theory as there can be the occasional exception. Lala companies don't care much about websites or email, depending instead on the Twitter account of the lala as the core of their digital strategy.

Culture: The lala takes all the decisions in the organization, and the rest of the employees are accustomed to blindly executing. The lala is always accompanied by his right-hand man, an understated shrewd accountant, dressed in trousers and a bush shirt and addressed by all as lastname-ji. Sometimes, families experiment by bringing in an outsider to lead the conglomerate but it usually fails, and they invariably end up bidding 'tata'. No one dares mess around in lala land.

Compensation: The pay is reasonable and the perks okay but if you align to the lala and lastname-ji, you are assured of lifelong employment. In this day and age, that is indeed quite something.

Functions

To efficiently control employees and prevent them from intermingling more than necessary, organizations group them into functions. If you think of a company as a farm, visualize all the cows being herded into a shed, horses in a stable, pigs in a sty, hens in a coop and so on. Once you settle on the kind of company that you would like to work for, you will need to select a function where you can spend the rest of your life comfortably slashing your wrists. Make your choice basis your inherent nature—for example, if you are a deer in headlights every time you encounter numbers, a marketing role would be right up your alley. If you have a chameleon-like ability to slip out of sticky situations, snag a career in sales. So which creature do you want to be?

Human Resources (HR)

HR deals with the organization's least important resource—people, and that's why it's not top of mind for most leaders or employees. Recall the classic *Sound of Music* scene with Maria on a mountain, gaily dancing hand in hand with the Von Trapp kids—everyone joyful, carefree and without a worry in the world. That's your typical HR department—a team with no real work, responsibilities or deliverables. Imagine having to come to work day after day merely to breathe! Well ok, they do handle some important tasks like conveying job requirements to recruitment consultants and printing and stapling resumes as they come in. They also occasionally deal with life and death crises such as a management trainee refusing a job offer at the last minute. But such periods of intense pressure are few and far between, and then, of course, there is the invariable headcount freeze when nothing is expected of them. Other than breathing.

One doesn't require a specialized degree, or any degree, to be a stellar HR professional. One simply needs a keen inclination for gossip and an inherent knack for leaking personal information. Occasional travel will be required to college campuses to bully graduating students, and the ability to use stationery and standard office equipment will be a huge plus.

Marketing

Snapping on the heels of HR for the best work–life balance are the folks in marketing. Their job is to fool customers into believing that the organization's product is not only required but also better than anyone else's. Even more impressive is that they pull this off from their ivory tower, without ever having met a customer or used the product themselves. To recognize a marketer, simply throw in a number in the middle of a sentence and watch his or her eyes glaze over. Marketers only communicate in images, stories and faff.

A degree in just about anything will suffice as long as you can articulate using jargon, and parrot market insights. You need to spend at least half the week in focus groups, conferences, events, team outings and movies. The marketing dress code is 'Business Dishevelled' and the messier you look, the more creative you are perceived to be. Lastly, you need a dispassionate personality to be completely detached from sales, the rest of the organization and the world at large.

Sales

Salespeople capitalize on the fictional propaganda created by Marketing to pull in the revenues. They get a lot of leeway therefore, and no one questions their whereabouts—one could be in bed or a matinee show but 'I was on a sales call' is a perfectly acceptable explanation. They are inexplicably the biggest consumers of visiting cards worldwide. Salespeople are of four kinds—the majority over-promise and under-deliver while a few under-promise and over-deliver. Then there are the exceptions who are too busy to make promises, and the rest who are too busy to deliver.

Anyone with the ability to lie shamelessly and with a thick skin to withstand constant criticism from bosses and clients will excel in sales. A large part of one's time will be spent warring with all departments and shifting the blame onto others; terrible interpersonal skills are therefore a prerequisite.

Finance

Finance looks after the money coming in and going out of the organization. They are also responsible for drafting draconian expense reimbursement policies that no one can conceivably adhere to. Finance professionals take a vow of celibacy along with their Chartered Accountancy final exam but get turned on by anything that resembles a spreadsheet. Be wary if you wear checked shirts or skirts around them. They are often uncharitably characterized as bean counters—people without any personality or vision who nit-pick through life moving from one financial planning cycle to the next. That is very apt.

Finance professionals are a rare breed of humans who are blessed with keen intelligence but without the trappings of common sense. It can, therefore, be extremely stimulating yet exasperating to deal with them. Add to that their complete lack of social skills and one can appreciate where this whole 'pounding one's head on the wall' move originated.

Operations and Technology (O&T)

The phrase 'think outside the box' was coined after researchers spent aeons observing Operations employees who could only think inside the box. Corporate workhorses with blinkers, they often confuse lateral with rudimentary toilets.

A function that thrives on customer aggravation rather than satisfaction, Operations is responsible for generating most of an organization's customer complaints. Their counterparts in Technology sit, trousers hitched at the waist, in a fortified room guarded by an access card and spend their time searching for a Server 404. One can only contact them by opening something called a ticket, a process which itself goes into an infinite loop because one needs to open a ticket to open a ticket. That's why all employees, including the people in O&T, hate the people in O&T.

One requires an extremely high level of incompetence to succeed here, but the good news is that you will be trained well. There are numerous examples of brilliant graduates who joined O&T departments and over time, worked their way down to the depths of ineptitude. One just needs to have patience and hopeless mentors, and in O&T, you will be rewarded with both.

Procurement and Administration

This function has critical organizational responsibilities such as ensuring that offices are clean and maintained, vendors paid on time, lease agreements signed and the company is getting a bang for its buck. It is also known as the 'amazing function' because it never fails to amaze people by the incredibly terrible deals it negotiates for the organization.

Procurement and Administration professionals model themselves on the Kauravas from Hindu mythology who sprawled around all day, played dice and bullied vendors. You will be given a personal beanbag, rulebooks for Ludo and Pachisi and the *Official Procurement & Admin's Guide to Crass Abuses* during orientation. You will also be brainwashed from concepts such as conscience and karma—to succeed here, you need to believe that all your daytime sins in office will be washed by the evening's whisky soda.

Audit and Risk

Kala Pani was a notorious cellular prison in the Andaman and Nicobar Islands where pre-Independence, the British exiled Indian political prisoners. Many perished while journeying to these remote islands; the rest were imprisoned and forgotten. Audit and Risk is the Kala Pani of corporate life. No one goes there voluntarily, and those who are banished there are either universally hated or consistently under-performing. Once there, they can crib and complain all they want, but no one cares.

Unfortunately, like the Count of Monte Cristo who escaped the *Chateau d'If* to take revenge on all his enemies, Kala Pani residents are let out once a year for a process called the annual audit. With a vengeance, they resurrect and unleash all that pent-up frustration—poring over documents, grilling folks and creating risks and issues where there are none. This is their payback, and you just need to stoically deal with it; soon, they will be back in the galley, rowing their way back to their island home.

To be a successful Audit and Risk professional, you need a sadomasochistic approach to work, anal attention to detail, a whiny voice and a stubbornly suspicious personality. Comfort with chains and ball gags are welcome assets.

Strategy / Research and Development (R&D)

Sometimes employees need a break from structured work and corporations have created Strategy and R&D departments for this purpose. You can move here and use your alleged expert skills to help develop future plans, products or services for the organization. Once you tire of goofing around, you can return to the real world of work.

Some R&D departments may require specialized skills, but generally, a transfer here is a reward for your contributions so far. Or a pre-emptive move to get you out before you cause serious damage in your current job. Either way, get those markers ready and prepare to doodle on whiteboards.

The Management Structure

Lastly, to exploit employees in a legally and socially acceptable fashion, they are placed in a hierarchical framework called the management structure. In its most elemental form, this structure comprises of **early careers** who have absolutely no authority in the organization, **middle management** who believe that they have some, and **senior leadership** who have it all. Your endeavour, over a lifetime of work, is to go from the first to the third level.

Early Careers: At the bottom of the corporate pyramid, these employees are relatively fresh into the workforce. They are intense, intelligent, impatient, industrious, irreverent and importantly, irrelevant. They are individual performers who care deeply about how they are perceived when ironically, absolutely no one cares.

Middle Management: At the crossroads of corporate life, these employees are too old to screw it up and too young to give it up. They get blamed if things go wrong and receive little credit if they don't. They have recently taken on the stress of managing people, and there is no work–life balance at a life stage where a busy partner, young children and ageing parents are pulling them in all directions. The organizational pyramid narrows hereon, with a lot of them vying for a few senior leadership positions. They are the squeeze-ball of office politics and stress.

Senior Leadership: Having clawed themselves out of the morass of middle management, these select few have hit the big league. They have large teams who do all the work and they just show up to take the credit. Their name is prominent in the 'About Us' section on the company's website, and they are the ones on stage at events, handing out not receiving awards. Their word is gospel, and they spend most of the day replying to emails with an 'Approved, regards'. They live in a mansion in the suburbs, the kids are heading to college and their second spouse is doing yoga, baking kale chips and ordering organic avocados.

YOUR FOOT IN
THE DOOR

I

HOW TO PEDDLE HOPE
Cracking interviews and group discussions

The CV

The first step to getting a great job is either to ask your powerful papa or prepare a kick-ass Curriculum Vitae (CV). Now if you had a resourceful parent, you would be busy riding his or her coat-tails instead of reading this book. So let's get to the more practical aspect of preparing CVs.

A CV summarizes your supposed skills and accomplishments and is designed to hoodwink prospective employers. You can include your photograph, marital status and vital statistics and call it a biodata; or give it an elegant Westernized touch by adding some accent marks and calling it a résumé. Irrespective, this brag sheet is nothing but your to-do list from the past—things that you should have accomplished in previous jobs but didn't. But the future always holds hope so go ahead and inflate your

3

achievements, using the helpful hints on this page, and pray that you get the interview call.

YOUR NAME

Contact details including a professional email ID; cutedimples1981@something.com is not advisable

Objective   Explain why you want to waste the next few years working in the hopeless company that you have applied to.

Education   SCHOOLS AND COLLEGES YOU HAVE ATTENDED
- List your degrees. Chances are that no one might've heard of the academic institutions you attended. So, tour the Harvard campus at some point in your life and position it as an executive MBA on your CV.
- Rephrase bad grades—'Consistently ranked in the top four quartiles' sounds much better than 'came last in class'.

Experience   YOUR JOBS
- List all the jobs you have held and a few bullets on your responsibilities and supposed achievements in each role. Start each bullet with an action verb:
  o <u>Led</u> some people in doing something
  o <u>Founded</u> some society to support something
  o <u>Spearheaded</u> some initiative to achieve something
- Imply that the company's success was thanks to your awesome contributions.

- o My expertise in geology helped me collect, analyze and overlay the ideal combination of rock and construction materials across a variety of multilane infrastructural projects in the Greater Mumbai catchment area. (I drove bulldozers)

- Pad long gaps in your CV with fictitious internships and projects done for friends and family.

Skills
- Anything that you can do can count as a special skill.
- Know how to answer the phone? Great oral communication.
- Able to read this sentence and partly understand what I am saying? Excellent comprehension.
- Own a watch? Extremely punctual.
- Use Microsoft Office? Expert in a range of productivity-enhancing software.
- Addicted to Snapchat? Extremely reliable and discreet professional.

Other Interests
- List anything that can spark off a conversation. Mention your hobby of collecting navel fluff and be prepared to talk about it at length.

References AVAILABLE UPON REQUEST
- Give names of some close friends and family members. Brief them on what they need to say if they are called and do a few dry runs.
- Feel free to list me as a reference; I have no doubt whatsoever that after reading this book, you will do the corporate world proud.

The Interview

An interview is essentially an opportunity for potential employers to evaluate whether you can lie as effectively in person as you do on paper. Don't let them down.

You don't get a second chance to make a first impression. People take less than a minute to form their views and simply spend the rest of the time validating their initial instinct. So don't mess it up. A firm handshake is critical and start extending your right hand as you walk in, lifting it a few degrees with each stride. Pace yourself such that it is perpendicular to your torso by the time you reach the interviewer. Grasp his hand, which is hopefully outstretched as well, and shake it firmly. In case he's oblivious to your friendly intentions, don't look silly with your extended palm and quickly raise it to brush imaginary gook off your hair, as if that was your original intent.

During the interrogation, you need to offer hope that you can accomplish whatever you have listed on your CV and they should be grinning with delight at your claims. Give yourself a point for each 'Ooooh' or 'Aaaah' that you can elicit from your interviewer and deduct a point for every eye roll. End with a positive score.

Many interviewers will judge you through behavioural questions that probe your past experiences to determine future reactions. Share an example of an important goal that you set and achieved or provide an example of the biggest risk you have taken—that sort of pretentious hooey. To prepare, you only need to be ready with about six stories, preferably true but in your case probably fictional, in the following genres:

Horror	A bloodcurdling apocalyptic tale around dire family circumstances, natural disasters and severe health issues that explains gaps in your CV or your pathetic academic performance
Action & Suspense	An edge-of-the-seat thriller about you successfully overcoming an intense, high pressure, tight deadline situation
War	A compelling sublime account about your leadership skills in resolving multiple conflicts that arose in a team environment
Fantasy & Sci-fi	A wild yarn about your lofty goals and aspirations for the future and your confidence in achieving them
Comedy & Romance	A warm and fuzzy fairy-tale about your inability to maintain adequate work–life balance and your partner's support in dealing with it
Drama	A tense, powerful and emotional saga about overcoming significant personal and professional challenges to become the person that you are

You can mix and match anecdotes from the above stories to answer most questions and wherever possible, include live demonstrations.

Interviewer: What would you consider to be your biggest weakness?

You: Umm ... I tend to be very secretive.

Interviewer: Really ... can you give an example?

You: No.

If the interviewer asks you the routine, 'Where do you see yourself a few years down the line?' politely tell him that it is none of his business and instead cross-examine him on his career plans. If he visualizes himself in the same job, you can kiss any hopes of professional advancement goodbye. It's more important that you have an ambitious boss rather than him having a focused employee.

Finally, most interviewers end by enquiring if you have any questions for them. Rather than sheepishly shaking your head, ask about their journey with the organization and then simulate slurping sounds as they drone on about their careers. Impress them with your fake interest. Alternatively, keep it simple, give a coy smile and ask, 'So ... when can I join?'

If you happen to be exploring opportunities with a competitor, keep things exciting and refuse to come into their office, suggesting that industry gossip will spread if you're spotted. Instead, meet in disguise at a coffee shop or park and share a predetermined code that will identify you, such as holding a newspaper and tapping your right foot. The higher the level of intrigue that you create, the more alluring your candidacy will be.

Finally, it's always a good strategy to inflict your questioner with CIFS (Chronic Interview Fatigue Syndrome). Have a bunch of under-qualified friends apply for the same position and go for their interviews before you. Once the interviewer has met a string of complete losers in quick succession, a nitwit like you will, in relative comparison, appear to be Einstein. The offer letter should get printed even as you are tapping that right foot.

Group Discussions

Some organizations put all candidates into a room and give them a case study—'How will the liberalization of foreign exchange controls impact currency markets?' or 'Would you cast Katrina or Kareena for a biopic on Kangana?' Via this exercise, they attempt to replicate the work environment and gauge superficial stuff such as intellect, interpersonal skills and teamwork.

Wing it.

Don't be the silent, angry young man in the background but register your presence early; say anything or just cough distinctively, but get those vocal chords warmed up. Supplement this with sage nodding as you observe the reactions of the panel and like a good commentator, keep making irrelevant but factual observations about whatever's happening around you. 'Everyone is talking at the same time—let's take it one by one.' Or, 'We have spent a lot of time on this one point. Let's move onto something else.'

Take on any one role that demonstrates responsibility to the panel—whether the timekeeper, note taker, whiteboard writer or coordinator. If you have nothing original to contribute, become the summarizer and frequently recap the discussion so far. 'Ok, so as things stand, we have discussed A, B and C.' It demonstrates that you are listening.

Manage confrontations smartly and pick your opponents based on the threat they pose to you getting the job. Harmless ideas should elicit, 'That's a good suggestion. I would add on to it with ...' The ones who are an obstacle between you and the appointment letter should be dissed,

'I disagree with my colleague whose impractical idea will not work in the real world.' Escalate tensions and put other candidates on the spot, 'Hey, you both are constantly disagreeing with each other. Do you want to share with us as to what the issue is?' And embarrass others with occasional jeers such as, 'Tara got roasted!' or, 'Raj got a burn!'

Remember that you don't have to lead the group all the time but merely show some leadership elements occasionally. Just like you would in office.

Tips for Interviewers

Always treat every candidate like scum; not because you are a bad person but you want to see how he reacts to what will be his inevitable future if he joins. Keep him waiting endlessly; patience is a virtue that he needs to develop from the start. Do not offer tea and coffee; that makes him alert and you want to catch him at his worst. Start with small talk around films he sees, books he reads, etc., so that you can make unwarranted judgements about him.

Interviews are stressful and you should up the tension a few notches. Start by attacking the weakest link in his CV and get him flustered early—'I notice you scored really badly in your tenth grade exams. Are you an imbecile?' Nod with boredom at his accomplishments and shake your head in disgust at any let-down. Make random notes as he speaks and let him wonder what you are noting down. Pull out your phone, start messaging, look up, smirk and continue messaging.

React violently when you don't like his answers and observe his reaction. Try to make him cry. If he can't handle you during the interview, how will he manage once he joins? The biggest favour you can do him is to replicate the experience of working with you as best as you can.

Campus Hiring

If interviewing on campus, you are competing with hundreds of companies. In a system probably unique to India, students are effectively compelled to accept the first job offer they receive. So you need to meet the best students as early as possible so they are forced to join your hopeless organization.

Now your interview slot depends on how aspirational your organization is—the most prestigious companies get slots on the first day of the recruitment cycle (the coveted Day 1), the next set gets Day 2 and so on. The losers end up around Day 7, by which time only the chaff is available. Unsurprisingly, there have been bitter tussles between corporates and colleges for Day 1 slots, so campuses slimily moved the clock back and introduced Day 0, a day of interviews before Day 1. Real heavy hitters were quietly moved to Day 0, and others were fooled into believing they were the crème de la crème Day 1 companies.

Ideally, skip this recruiting week nonsense altogether and target Day (a few years) slots by joining the college's admissions committee. That way, you can make job offers to candidates as their applications for admission come in.

In Conclusion...

It is the best interviewee and not the best candidate who gets the job; just figure out what the employer needs and peddle hope that you can deliver. Keep honing the art of effective interviewing and you should be able to pick from the choicest of positions. Even if this is the only skill you have, your career will stay in great shape. Interview like a star, get hired, screw up and as soon as you sense an imminent firing, repeat cycle.

FEEL GOOD ANECDOTES

The chefs who cooked up their CVs

There are umpteen instances where corporate honchos have exaggerated their resumes, only to be eventually caught out and go down in flames. Former Yahoo CEO Scott Thompson claimed that he had a degree in accounting, which he did, and in computer science, which he didn't. Jack Grubman, Wall Street's highest paid analyst at the time at an annual compensation of $20 million, lied about attending MIT, when in fact he was at the nearby Boston University. Jeffrey Papows, a president at IBM, fibbed about getting his PhD from Pepperdine University when he actually got it via correspondence from an unaccredited school.

And then we have Robert Irvine, an established celebrity chef with hit shows and bestselling books until his imagination got the better of his cooking. He claimed that he was knighted by the Queen with the Knight Commander of the Royal Victorian Order—the highest level possible and gifted a castle in Scotland. He took credit for the wedding cake of Prince Charles and Lady Diana—a 360 fruitcake where he apparently carved tales of the history of the Windsor and Spencer families in icing. In reality, he helped pick out the fruit that would go on it. He asserted that he had received a degree from the University of Leeds whereas he simply attended a programme organized by the Navy. He maintained that he had served presidents and heads of state at the White House—he actually trained military cooks. We are unsure about his food but the cooking up of his CV surely deserves a few Michelin stars.

And meet Chef Ronnie Seaton who allegedly spent thirty-two years in the White House cooking for five presidents and published a tell-all book about his experiences. According to him, Ronald Reagan loved his food, George Bush was referred to as Daddy Bush, he would hear slaps whenever Hillary Clinton lashed out at Bill, and he uncovered a one-night stand between George W. Bush and then Secretary of State Condoleezza Rice. He also claimed to have cooked the most seductive meal ever for Bill Clinton and Monica Lewinsky on the night of their fateful encounter. In his book, *Sir White House Chef*, he describes the state of the room and the dress Monica was wearing.

'Ooh, that dress,' I commented. 'It's really long.'

'Yeah, we have to take it to the cleaners,' the man answered. 'It's got a stain on the chest.'

'A stain?' I didn't think much about it.

He ups the ante by claiming to have cooked so delicious a meal for the visiting Queen of England that she sought him in the kitchen and pleaded for the recipes. Not just that, she summoned him to Buckingham Palace to cook Christmas dinner, after which she was so smitten that she knighted him on the spot.

I looked up at her and asked, 'What did you just do?'

'I knighted you. You are now a Knight of my realm.'

'But I'm not from England, Your Majesty,' I cried.

'Your meal was so impressive that I had to do this for you.'

The White House has no record of him working there, Buckingham Palace has nothing on his knighthood and Cornell University is unaware about his claimed Doctorate in 'Foodology'. When a reporter asked him for proof to back up his White House experience claim, he responded, 'I can see what my wife has in the file cabinet.' Once the story broke, his publishers pulled the book out of stores though it might have been easier to simply move them to the fiction section.

The British Blundering Company

If you think your job interviews are stressful, wait till you hear what these Guys went through.

The British Broadcasting Company (BBC)—the global benchmark for journalistic rigour—was reporting on an important case that Apple had just lost. Noted technology expert Guy Kewney was invited to their studio for a live interview on the ground-breaking judgement. Kewney, an articulate Caucasian Londoner, arrived at the BBC office and was asked to wait in, let's call it, Reception Room 1 (RR1). Independently, an obscure technology department at BBC had posted some open data cleansing positions, and French speaking applicant Guy Goma, native of Guyana, arrived for that interview and was made to wait in, let's say, Reception Room 2 (RR2).

Guy Kewney was scheduled to go on air and a staffer came to RR2 and enquired, 'Are you Mr Guy, here for the interview?' Up sprang Goma, résumé safely tucked in his file folder and he was quickly whisked to the studio.

Kewney waited impatiently in RR1.

The staffer made a stop for make-up and a bewildered Mr Goma was patted down with rouge, powder and all the other cosmetics that come on before a live telecast. It's probably a whacky BBC protocol, he thought, and mentally rehearsed answers to the toughest data cleansing questions that he could think of. 'The guest seems a little stressed,' the staffer walkie-talkied to the news anchor, who made a mental note to put him at ease. Nervous perspiration sufficiently masked by powder, Goma marched into the studio.

Kewney was still waiting impatiently in RR1.

Goma sat in front of the cameras, beads of sweat forming again under the glare of the arc lights. The interviewer flashed him a warm smile and turning to the camera, gushed, 'We are pleased to have with us Mr Kewney, editor of the technology website, News Wireless.' While not a native English speaker, Goma understood enough to know that he was in hot broadcast soup and rolled his eyes and gulped nervously.

Kewney, still waiting impatiently in RR1, heard his name on the TV set on the wall and turned in horror to watch a stranger impersonating him.

The anchor started with a softball asking Goma if he was surprised at the Apple verdict. 'Yes, I am very surprised to be here, I wasn't really expecting this,' he said truthfully, very clearly not understanding the question. The anchor didn't understand the answer either and moved on to her next question, 'Do you think more people will now download music online?' 'Now that I'm screwed, let me enjoy this,' he probably thought, and Guy dived head-first into the discussion, giving unintelligible answers on his vision of the future of music downloads.

Kewney continued watching in RR1—now more amused than aghast.

Goma's answers were leaving the anchor, the audience as well as Goma himself, more confused than enlightened and the interview was hurriedly wrapped up. The mistake was eventually discovered, Kewney given a profuse apology and Goma packed off to his actual data cleansing interview, which unfortunately didn't go too well either and he didn't get the job. But he did become an overnight sensation in the media circuit in UK.

(View the interview online by searching for 'BBC News blunder Guy Goma'.)

The handshake hool

Russian Prime Minister Dmitry Medvedev is an expert when it comes to recovering from the handshake hool—the tricky manoeuvre where your counterpart ignores your outstretched hand. His sublime skill was apparent when Fijian Prime Minister Voreqe Bainimarama paid him a visit in 2013. Dmitry welcomed him with an open and outstretched palm which Bainimarama promptly ignored to shake hands with Medvedev's aides instead. Without missing a beat, Medvedev recovered and proceeded to dust imaginary dust from his jacket sleeve.

Slickly done, Dmitry. Slickly done.

(Watch the handshake hool online, preferably in slow motion for better learning, by searching for 'Bainimarama meets Medvedev'.)

The ultimate reference check

It is understandable when friends and family lie through their teeth to help get you a job but what would a complete stranger do if he were asked to provide you with a fake reference? Australian comedy duo Hamish and Andy decided to test this out by dialling a random stranger, live on radio, and asking him to provide a reference for someone he had never met.

First, Hamish arbitrarily called and reached James Lord, a twenty-three-year-old electrician from Melbourne, and introduced himself as Tim Barnard, someone who was just stepping in for an accounting job interview. He needed a last-minute reference and he told James that he had simply listed his number as one. He pleaded with James to cover up just in case someone happens to call him. 'Yeah sweet, I'll just tell them that you're a ripper bloke—I've got you covered,' said James confidently.

About ten minutes later, Andy called James, pretending to be from the accounting firm that Tim had interviewed with and acted as if he was checking on Tim's references. And what followed was an ovation-worthy exchange with James going overboard to enhance the reputation of a person he had never met. He created fictional examples to demonstrate that Tim would do a stellar job in accounting, citing personal instances of the fundraisers Tim had helped him with. He made him out to be a multilingual go-getter who always gets things done. Andy finally tried to stump James by asking him to describe the physical features of someone he had spoken to for a few moments on the phone. Without missing a beat, he answered with the diplomatic, 'Well, what you see is what you get with him.'

If you are listing phony references in your CV, make sure they match up to the standards set by legends such as James Lord.

(The hilarious segment can be viewed online by searching for 'Andy Hamish Job reference'.)

2

WELL BEGUN IS HALF DONE
Setting expectations and lowballing goals

You have accepted the offer, cleared the medicals, bought a new outfit, updated your LinkedIn profile, congratulated yourself with a 'feeling humbled' post on Facebook, and are ready to embark on a new journey. Amateur professionals try to hit the ground running and waste time in preparing for the role by doing background reading, meeting people, etc. It's the honeymoon period and they want to make a great impression on their boss and score some quick wins. 'Professional' professionals, on the other hand, are in no rush to drop their wedding ensembles, focusing instead on setting the tone for the relationship in the early days. Manage the honeymoon period well and the marriage will not be as unhappy.

Setting Expectations

The topmost priority is to set expectations right. Start with basics such as understanding the landscape of the office and locating the rest rooms, coffee machines, printers and exits. Much of your career will be spent idling here so quickly get a lay of the land. Scope out where the boss sits and map the best routes to the above destinations without crossing his workspace.

Ingrain the bad habits before it is too late to unlearn them. For example, don't come in to office too early lest your boss believes that you are an early morning person. Don't turn in work before the deadline but wait for a few gentle reminders —you have a long procrastinating career ahead of you and let him appreciate that you aren't very tardy. Answer back the first few times you get yelled at to firmly establish that you are no pushover. Make the extra effort to be who you are not so that eventually he gladly accepts who you are.

Quickly decode the power structures; while an organizational chart will give you a sense of the formal hierarchy, the actual power centres can be very different. Use your orientation meetings and informal lunches and eavesdrop in corridors to determine who the real power brokers are. You need to uncover the influencers who have the management's ear, the perception destroyers who can injure with their gossip and the politicians who can stab you with a smile. Associate with the right crowd and weasel into these groups as quickly as you can.

While aligning to your supervisor is critical, the shelf sitters are equally important. They are the old geezers, past their prime but still hanging around, thanks to the former contributions they have made to the organization. They are identifiable by their senior titles, huge cabins, matronly executive assistants and lack of direct responsibility for anything. No one talks to them or pays heed to their suggestions and you should capitalize on their need for attention by snagging one of these fossils as a mentor. There's nothing to lose—Gramps can't destroy your career any faster than you would on your own but he just might take an interest in you and help with networking and recommendations. So, wrangle your way into his dismal life.

Work vs Accountability

Early in your career, establish a reputation as an enthusiastic eager beaver, always willing to take on more responsibilities. You have a distinct advantage as people will believe your claim that you want to work harder. Alarms would go off if a mid-manager were to do this—why does he want more responsibilities, is he not busy enough, is he making a case for a promotion, is he trying to take the boss's job? And the person would be shunted out of the cabin with a laundry list of improvement areas expected in his current role. However, people expect you to have unlimited energy, time and willingness to learn and the best way to demonstrate that is to pretend to seek more work.

Now you might be worried that you will indeed get burdened with more work if you ask for it. Netflix and chill. Merely pretending to do a task is different from being accountable, where you are responsible for the task that needs to be done. You are too junior to be answerable for anything, so it's completely fine if your to-do list expands indefinitely.

Transitioning In

If you are moving into a new job, you are given a window of opportunity called the 'transitioning in' period that can last as much as a few months. During this time, the organization expects you to settle in and gives a lot more leeway than it usually might. Many business gurus have written claptrap on making the most of your first few months; ignore everything and simply run a five-pronged SMEAR campaign for your transition.

Sabotage

Keep the starting point of your performance measurement as low as possible—the more screwed up things are when you start, the easier it is to show improvement. So irrespective of how good or bad the situation really is, declare it completely botched up and set rock bottom expectations with the seniors. Then use the next few months to mess up matters further so that the bar is not just low—it's underground.

Malign

A transition is one of the few periods in your career where you aren't the problem but the solution and blame your predecessor for everything. He created all the issues and make him your punching bag. The bad decisions, state of the business, his lack of focus as he was transitioning out—it's all his fault. Keep it diplomatic though as you don't want to come across as a whiner, 'I don't really want to blame anyone who isn't here to defend his decisions, but I can't fathom why he would have chosen to do that...'

Equivocate

Now get onto the task of being absolutely ambiguous and non-committal on your course of action. Keep everyone hanging. Under promise with the intent of over delivering. Give your seniors the faith that you will fix things in one year and then go ahead and do it in ten months. It won't be difficult because it shouldn't even have taken a week—there was no mess to fix other than what you created.

Assess

By now, you are probably struggling with what exactly you are supposed to be doing in this job. You can't ask your boss since that's what he hired you for in the first place. Inquire with others—your team, colleagues, customers, suppliers, partners, distributors and anyone who is familiar with any aspect of your role. Don't seek explicit advice—position it more as a casual 'If you were in my shoes, what would you be doing?' question. Be outwardly dismissive of whatever they say but keep mental notes. If so many people would do those things if they were in your shoes, you should seriously consider it ... because you are.

Revamp

Finally, show some immediate action and make some changes in the team, whether required or not. Sack a few people and rejig some portfolios—anything to create a flutter. It keeps people on their toes and they will rush to align with you. If you don't know who to penalize, go after the people who seem most loyal to your predecessor. You don't want operatives putting a spanner in your 'blame the previous manager' works.

End the SMEAR campaign with a grand 'We are the Change' drive where you give everyone in your department 'We are the Change' caps and T-shirts and put up colourful posters all over the office. Good professionals always get everyone to rally around the imaginary problems that they have created.

Goal-Setting

Whether starting a new job or year, you will go through the charade of setting goals. As Napoleon Hill noted, a goal is a dream with a deadline. In the corporate scenario, the dream happens to be documented and your future depends on how you are perceived to have performed against it.

Quantifiable goals are based on the prior period's performance and your seniors will try set revenue targets significantly higher than what you delivered and expense targets much lower. Your objective should be to pad these goals as much as possible. Understate your projected revenues by painting dire scenarios of the economy—your outlook must be dismal. Inflate expected expenses by budgeting for one-off items such as marketing campaigns or technology—you won't spend the money but get the budgets anyway and then show them as savings at year-end. You should be hedging more vigorously than a schizophrenic stock trader.

Non-quantifiable goals are easier to manipulate and keep things as vague as possible. Insert fuzzy objectives like 'maintain a strong control environment', 'ensure camaraderie between departments', 'launch customer centric products', etc. Your boss will push you to quantify some of this but resist; as the cliché goes, what can be measured can be managed and you don't want to be subjected to either. So, keep your goals ambiguous, indefinite and ill defined.

In Conclusion...

The enthusiasm that most people feel at starting a new job, while understandable, is completely unwarranted and must be curbed. Because it's only a matter of time before you start hating your co-workers, plotting the demise of your boss and updating your CV. But a job well begun is more than half done and since you probably won't complete it anyway, a good start is even more important. Flirt coquettishly and set the right expectations. Just because the marriage will eventually end in divorce doesn't mean that you shouldn't enjoy the honeymoon.

 FEEL GOOD ANECDOTES

One of the most successful demonstrations of an effective SMEAR campaign comes from American politics. Donald Trump, US President at the time of writing, and a role model who epitomizes numerous *Job Be Damned* attributes, took over from Barack Obama in January 2017. His first 90 days, where he claimed that 'no administration has accomplished more' displayed all the classic attributes of a highly effective transition period.

Sabotage: Trump started setting rock bottom expectations long before he even became president. He declared every aspect of America—the economy, immigration, law and order—completely broken. And true to form, he proceeded to sabotage whatever he had inherited as soon as he took office. He messed up immigration acts, botched medical aid reform and annoyed a plethora of world leaders. He made things so bad that he ended his transition period with the lowest approval rating of any president ever.

Malign: Trump was maligning Obama even while campaigning and he wasted no time as the movers were unpacking bathrobes in the Lincoln bedroom. He called Obama the founder of terror group ISIS, one of the worst negotiators ever and blamed him for stoking protests and even wiretapping his offices. He labelled Obama possibly the worst president in the history of the country and responsible for the apparent chaos that Trump inherited.

Equivocate: Having efficiently messed things up, Trump displayed fantastic skill in being non-committal on his future course of action. According to the *Washington Post*, three months into his term, Trump had not started work on 60 per cent of his campaign promises and had already broken five of them. The way he was going, no one had a clue about what he will achieve during his presidency. Which is exactly how it should be.

Assess: With no prior experience in government, Trump was gasping like a fish out of water. He probably asked his confidants on what they would do if they were in his shoes but apparently, no one had the guts to tell him to resign.

Revamp: Trump conducted a text book revamping of the team and replaced anyone who was remotely a threat with close friends and family, who were loyally clueless. The acting Attorney General was fired for letting him know that his whacky travel ban was illogical and illegal. All foreign ambassadors were sacked without having replacements in place. And not only officials from the previous administration, he also fired staff who he had himself recently appointed. When it came to creating utter confusion, he was unbeatable.

Trump ran a classic SMEAR transition campaign. Expectations were set so low that if he manages to get through his term without setting off World War III, he will go down in history as a true legend.

3

METEOROLOGICAL GUIDE TO BOSS MANAGEMENT

Understanding, aligning and sucking up

However one approaches theology, a seeker will find that all paths invariably lead to one God. In the corporate world, this single power has different names—*jefe* in Spanish, *patron* in French, *chef* in German, *laoban* in Chinese and mai-baap in Hindi. But he is the One—the ultimate authority who you report to. In English-speaking countries, he is simply known as the Boss.

A job would have been perfect if not for two aspects—work and bosses. Your boss's primary role is to watch you work while your basic objective is to avoid work and this is the fundamental conflict. This is why managing him is essential and here's a three-step process to get this done.

Step 1: Understanding

Boss management has its roots in meteorology, the study of climate and weather.

Climate

This is the generally prevailing weather condition of a region—temperature, pressure, humidity, averaged over a series of years. When it comes to bosses, the climate equates to their overall temperament and disposition. Are they short-tempered or patient, taskmasters or relaxed, hyperactive or Zen-like? The boss's climate is influenced by various factors such as upbringing, past jobs, family, etc., and to have an enduring relationship, you need to understand it.

Research the heck out of him—his sports, hobbies, wives, mistresses. While he thinks that you are working, you should instead be probing, fact finding and gathering every piece of personal information that you can. Grill people who have worked for him in the past and stalk him on social media. Let your colleagues do all the tedious office work. Information is power and stay focused on accumulating it.

Weather

While climate is long term, the weather describes the immediate prevailing conditions. It is transient and frequently changes. The weather, in boss management, equates to his current mood—is he happy, angry, sad or relaxed? And just as one checks external conditions before embarking on a trip, you should assess his weather before engaging with him.

Given the impact weather can have on your career, pay heed to the newscaster—your boss's executive assistant. She can alert you as required—are the skies clear or cloudy this morning? Can you expect slight precipitation when you walk in with your overdue project or heavy showers with thunder?

She also controls his calendar. Stay on her right side as she can reschedule meetings, or share his travel schedule to help you plan your days off. Of all your relationships, invest the most heavily in this one and buy her gifts on her birthday, wish her on festivals, respond promptly to her follow ups and never make her wait. Build your bridges on strong pillars of flattery with her at the earliest.

Step 2: Alignment

We are attracted to people who we believe are just like us. Once you have a good understanding of your boss's interests, likes and dislikes, align with him by becoming who he'd like you to be, essentially his clone.

Replicate his physical characteristics starting with his hairstyle—does he part to the left or to the right? Shamelessly copy. Is he bald? Get those shears out. Then begin dressing, talking, walking, sitting and doing everything like him— does he lift a bum or let it loose on the cushion? Adapt your style accordingly. Have you ever been to a venture capital or private equity gathering—it's like walking into a hall of mirrors—everyone looks and acts identically. But that is precisely the reason that they are all so successful.

Next, identify all commonalities with your boss that your climactic research unearthed. Do you both like the same actors or a similar genre of music? Do you follow the same sports teams? Even if there are no similarities, create some. Fake an appreciation for Air Supply just because the honcho gets off to '*Making love out of nothing at all*'. Google map the heck out of his birthplace and claim to have also grown up there. Anything that you both have in common can help immensely in forging a bond.

Like any good pyramid scheme developer, don't limit yourself to the top dog but align with everyone affiliated with him. Stay in the good books of anyone who he depends on—you want them to praise you in their private conversations with him. Likewise, compliment him to those who might relay the information back as there is nothing better than him getting a whiff of your adulation indirectly rather than straight from you.

There is no upside to dissonance and vociferously agree with him on anything he says and then do nothing. He will be so caught up dealing with the people who disagreed that he won't notice your lack of action. And if he does, simply agree that you have done nothing, apologize, and then do nothing again.

While you should never forget that you are little more than cow dung stuck to his Oxfords, alignment works both ways. Keep him alert by occasionally dropping the names of industry headhunters who are supposedly stalking you for competitive jobs. Or spread a rumour throughout the organization that you have a special relationship with your boss's boss and if he probes, smile cryptically without confirming or denying. The best alignment is like a good ballet performance—everyone on their toes all the time.

Step 3: Sucking Up

Understanding the boss is the foundation on which solid careers are built and aligning to him is the strategic aspect of career growth. The final leg, sucking up, is tactical and involves making the right moves from time to time. Meritocracy is a silly notion that only exists in corporate websites; it is only the lickspittles who get ahead. One gets better with age and experience and the more time you spend in the workforce, the more effectively you will brown nose your way up the ladder.

Proactiveness is a prerequisite for effective backscratching and be quick and gung-ho about anything that concerns him. Be the first to organize a cake for his birthday and let him know that it was all your doing. Treat the team to an inexpensive pedestrian meal or outing and allow news of your generosity to reach him. Offer to cover up for him if he needs to get away and suggest that he takes a day off, even if he doesn't. Anticipate his needs and stay a step ahead, he will forever appreciate it.

A good suck up is one that doesn't feel like flattery to the person you are apple-polishing. Disguise blatant compliments such as 'Sir, you have awesome negotiation skills' as guidance seeking pleas, 'Maestro, I loved the way you negotiated that deal. Can you advise me on this transaction I am working on?'

The meal at home is a winner. Have your spouse geared up for an evening of polite conversation and the kids spruced up and ready to recite poetry. If the top gun is bringing along his queen bee, remember that the corporate organization structure is mirrored at home—if you are one-down to the boss, your spouse is, by default, one-down to his spouse. You can helpfully draw out a spousal organizational chart so that she is crystal clear on the straight and dotted line relationships that she has with other spouses in the organization.

Finally, never make any Career Limiting Moves (CLMs) that have the potential to bring your career to an abrupt halt. Don't get drunk and grab hold of his collar at a party, get caught making out with his wife or upgrade yourself to business class while he flies in economy. Save any bravado for retirement.

Change of Guard

There are few things as stressful in corporate life as getting a new boss. A change of guard topples the entire comfort zone ecosystem that you painstakingly built with his predecessor. Its taken a long time to fine-tune your sycophancy, operate at his wavelength and adjust your body clock to his office timings and suddenly, you have to reset the whole damn thing. Also, people prefer to have handpicked rather than inherited underlings so you are disadvantaged anyway. And if he happens to be a co-worker or anyone you've rubbed the wrong way in the past, you're screwed with a capital F; give him seventy-two hours to settle down before he starts settling old scores.

Quickly restart the three-step process of boss management. And apologize for any wrongdoings of the past, blame any previous goof-ups to instructions of your previous supervisor and swear undying loyalty to the new chief. It's either your job or your dignity at stake and it's a straightforward choice.

In Conclusion...

Quite like your parents, you cannot choose your bosses and they are an unavoidable aspect of corporate life. The best you can do is to align with them so they stay diverted while you pretend to work. Amateur professionals often make the mistake of assuming that if the boss looks good, they will also shine as in his success lies their own. Hilarious. The supervisor-subordinate relationship is a perpetual high-stakes game of who blinks first and the first person to make an organizational blunder loses. So just wait patiently till he eventually makes a misstep because as long as he screws up before you, you are sorted.

FEEL GOOD ANECDOTES

While we would like to believe that no one has it worse than us when it comes to bosses, there is no shortage of eccentric tyrants in the corporate world.

Kisses are in vogue

It's nice if bosses encourage friendship amongst employees but Richard 'Mad Dog' Beckman, publisher at *Vogue*, took his need for camaraderie to a whole new level.

Wrapping up a staff meeting at *Vogue's* L.A. offices, he had this sudden intense desire to see two women make out. So he grabbed the head of his West Coast ad director Carol and shoved it into the face of international fashion director Emily in an effort to make them koochie koochie. So sudden and violent was his move that Carol's nose and cheekbone slammed into Emily's forehead with such force that she required severe reconstruction surgery. Randomly smooching colleagues not really being part of her job description, Carol sued Condé Nast for $10 million. The suit was settled out of court and the world got yet another reason to validate Beckman's sobriquet of 'Mad Dog'.

He was let off easy and asked to apologize and undergo counselling. Hopefully, he didn't try to force his team of counsellors to be friends.

An absolute nut job

Korean Air's New York to Seoul flight was ready for take-off and attendant Kim Do-hee was stationed in First Class. Just as she had been instructed to do all through training, she went around the cabin and coyly served drinks and macadamia nuts to the passengers. Little did she know that a massive disastrophe was about to sweep over the flight.

Seated in first class was Heather Cho, a vice president at Korean Air and the daughter of the chairman. And boy, she went nuts when she saw that Kim had served her the snack in its original packaging rather than on a plate. Cho shrieked, abused, ranted and raved about this gross lapse in service. Kim and her boss, cabin crew chief Park Chang-jin were forced to kneel in front of her and apologize while she rapped their knuckles with a digital tablet. She then ordered the plane to return to the gate so that the chief could be offloaded while 250 passengers were made to wait. It was one of the biggest tantrums the world had seen, Oppa Gangnam style.

As is the norm the world over when spoiled brats get caught out, the affected parties were intimidated and witnesses bribed. A co-passenger who complained was sent a calendar and model aeroplane as an apology. But the incident still leaked, causing a global hue and cry. Ms Cho even eventually served a few months in prison where the wardens were extra careful in serving her meals. And at the time of writing, she is all set to return to a senior executive role, sending employees all across the chaebol into a collective shudder.

Please remember this the next time your boss asks you to pass the chana chor garam when you are out drinking.

We still have it better than our grandparents

This generation seems better off than workers in the last century.

John Patterson, founder of NCR (National Cash Register Company) was widely renowned as one of corporate America's pioneering sales management gurus. He was also a control, health and cleanliness freak mandating that employees have showers as per specified schedules during working hours and banning foods he didn't like from the cafeteria. Regular weigh-ins were conducted and underweight employees were given free malted milk. He would allegedly sack and then rehire employees to break their self-esteem. He even sacked one of his executives by putting his desk on the company's lawn and then setting it ablaze; this is probably where the phrase 'to get fired' originated.

And finally, we have Henry Clay Frick, chairman of Carnegie Steel and regarded as the father of the steel industry. He also held the title of the most hated man in America. While he and his partner Andrew Carnegie were raking in the moolah by the steel bucket, the poor union was crumbling under the burden of low wages and inflation. When they did the logical thing that most unions would do and asked him for a raise, he instead lowered their salaries. And when they did the next logical thing that most unions would do and went on strike, he literally set up an army to destroy them.

He installed sniper towers in his mills, set up barbed wire fencing, got in canons to fire boiling water and even recruited mercenaries to fight on his behalf. In the subsequent Homestead Strike of 1892, one of the worst labour disputes in American history, a full pitched battle occurred and dozens of people lost their lives and many more were injured.

And what is the worst that your boss does, flings some papers on the ground in anger?

THE HOLY TRINITY
OF WORK

4

MEETINGS: AN ACCEPTABLE ALTERNATIVE TO WORK

Strategies to be a rock star in every meeting

It's common practice for employees, in offices around the world, to gather around in a room for never-ending discussions on nothing in particular. These events are called meetings and they are a completely acceptable alternative to work, and you will rarely get castigated for participating. They do tend to generate follow-up work and therefore are the first leg of the holy trinity of Meetings-Procrastination-CYA.

Meetings are also a political minefield with participants using this communal forum to boost their profiles. Given your limited aptitude and expertise, your primary objective should be to come out unscathed and with your reputation intact. A single goof-up can scar you for life as a corporate dunderhead. But as you gain experience and confidence, you can start to go on the offensive and destroy your opponents. We will develop strategies to both make you look good and your colleagues look bad.

Pre-meeting Preparations

If at all you have a choice, don't participate in every meeting—feign illness, create a last-minute crisis or give any excuse to duck and send a colleague or subordinate instead. The more representatives there are attending meetings on your behalf, the less accountability you'll have and everything can be attributed to miscommunication and 'lines getting crossed'. Another effective way to scuttle invites is to insist that some other folks from different departments attend as well. The convener will go crazy coordinating multiple schedules and the meeting will never take place.

The Setting is Important

If you do go for a meeting, prepare thoroughly as every aspect of the experience is crucial. People tend to be happier and more cooperative when the weather is good, so postpone important meetings if it's dark and cloudy. Sugar increases glucose levels, generates warmth and makes people want to reciprocate your generosity; take pastries and coffee for everyone.

On the other hand, if you are unprepared, keep the meetings unwieldy by inviting more participants than the room can accommodate. The more people you have leaning uncomfortably against the wall, the faster they'll want it to end. And the more irrelevant people who attend, the more the opinions and consequently, lesser the time to focus on the items that you are unprepared for. Completely fill up the room and if you are short of attendees, dress up the pantry boys in shirts and ties and pass them off as interns.

As is the Seating

Be cognizant of location. Avoid the hot seat, diagonally opposite the boss, as that's where his attention will be focused. If you expect to contribute sensibly, grab the seat adjoining the hot seat and counterbalance the idiot getting roasted. You are adjacent to the boss and he will notice you nodding in agreement and scribbling notes. Occasionally lean in and whisper something intelligent. If you aren't prepared, pick a spot where it's impossible for the boss to make eye contact, such as the far end of the table with enough people separating you both. If he can't see you, he can't pick on you.

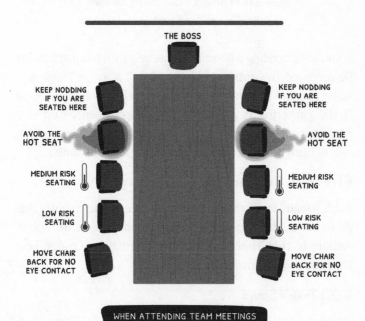

Create an imbalance of power by playing with the seating arrangements. A day prior, adjust the seat heights of all chairs, but one, to lower positions and sabotage them so that they wobble. Researchers have determined that shorter awkward chairs reduce testosterone and increase cortisol thereby reducing the feeling of power while you, seated on the one perfect chair, rule the room.

The Meeting Participation Formula

The number of points you need to make in a meeting is a function of its duration and participation.

$$\text{Number of points} = \text{Length of meeting} / (2 \times \text{number of participants})$$

If you are attending a 60-minute meeting with ten participants, be prepared to contribute about $60 / (2 \times 10) = 3$ points to be registered as an intelligent and effective contributor. If the gathering is cosier, you obviously need to up your contribution—a 30-minute meeting with three participants will require that you make $30 / (2 \times 3) = 5$ good points.

Effective Communication Strategies

Mark Twain wisely said, 'Better to keep your mouth shut and appear stupid than to open it and remove all doubt.' Adhere to this. However, when you do have to speak, keep the following pointers in mind.

Don't Take a Stand

Present both sides of an argument, without any recommendations, and let everyone mull over it. 'The pros of doing this are A, B, C, but on the other hand, the cons are X, Y, and Z.' Perfect the art of masterful inactivity and be the wise savant presenting an unbiased summary of the problem at hand. Wait until someone else makes the mistake of taking a stand and immediately start playing the devil's advocate, identifying all weaknesses before dismissing him.

Use Corollaries

Rephrase statements with 'So, if I hear you correctly ...' followed by its corollary. If the sales head declares victory with a proud 'We have achieved 40 per cent market share in the past quarter,' rephrase it as, 'So, if I hear you correctly, 60 per cent of the market is still buying competitor products.' If the operations head claims, 'We achieved 99 per cent accuracy in our processing last month,' retort with, 'So, if I hear you correctly, we screwed up one out of every 100 transactions.' While this may create some bad blood with colleagues, your boss will hear you correctly as a lateral thinker.

Discuss What's Already Known

People like to discuss stuff that they are already familiar with (shared information bias). Steer conversations towards popular topics and events. The time and energy of the group should be spent discussing matters that everyone already knows rather than subjects that are new to them. So, spending the entire meeting reviewing the minutes of the last one is an excellent idea.

Share Unrelated Personal Information

Researchers have found that disclosing unrelated personal information helps build trust, better rapport and makes your counterparts less aggressive. Throw in an unrelated titbit or two during meetings. 'Just wanted to share that I prefer to use my toilet paper folded up like a newspaper, unlike my wife who rolls it into an untidy ball.'

Language and Body Language

Use the appropriate language and gestures to create the right perceptions.

Being Warm and Inclusive

Create a sense of solidarity and responsibility by using inclusive language with colleagues, especially when your seniors are listening. 'Diligent executives like you and me never really worry about going the extra mile.' Be like Hephaestus, the Greek God of fire, blacksmiths, carpenters, and use warm, fuzzy, construction-oriented phrases that project an image of you doing manual labour for the good of the organization. 'Let's build the foundation,' 'Let's put the blocks in place,' and so on. Make eye contact and think of something pleasant—chocolates, rose gardens, falling rain, sex—anything that brings a smile to your face as you talk. If you imagine something pleasurable, your body will react similarly and you will come across as honest and sincere.

Being Confident and Powerful

Use high-octane action verbs to describe even the most mundane office tasks. I'm going to jump on a call, shoot a mail, drill down into the problem or am running late. It sounds so much more action-oriented than I'll join a call or send you a mail. Add some light swearing to sound passionate and persuasive—'Is there any one effing reason you cannot do this on time?' Occasionally refer to yourself in the third person, as if you are playing 'Simon says', to sound powerful. 'Rishi says do this project by the end of day.'

Wave your hands passionately with fingers wide as you make an important point. Add on some head clucking movements, back and forth like a chicken, and you'll surely receive the passionate Employee of the Month award. Hit the table hard a few times as you speak and it just got upgraded to Employee of the Year.

Don't use words and phrases that convey uncertainty, such as 'I think', 'I hope', etc. Don't round off numbers but instead be as precise as you can. Saying 'It will take us twenty-two months to be profitable,' is a lot more advantageous to you than 'I think it will take us around two years to be profitable.'

Pauses project confidence, so pause every time you want something construed as awesome, giving the audience time to process your stunning inferences. Pause before you answer a question, as if you are deep in thought and before emphasizing a particularly important word, 'Everyone is going to get (long pause) fired.' Pour yourself some water as you speak. The act of water pouring out from the bottle should be perfectly synchronized with your speech. Then take a sip, then a pause—it looks very dignified.

Switch Speech Styles

Occasionally, confuse the audience by switching from English to Shakespearean. 'Hark, thy speech is odorous and thee maketh points that hath no virtue.' You will look distinguished and well read. Or capitalize on the rhyme as reason effect where something is judged as more accurate and truthful when it is communicated in rhyme.

Just when every door in my career seemed to be slammed
Like a beacon of hope, came Job Be Damned

Nod Effectively

A nod is a very useful weapon in your corporate armoury. There is a difference between listening and hearing—listening in meetings requires that you pay attention while hearing simply requires that you nod to signal that you are attentive. Pace your nods to every few minutes and limit the range of head movement to about 15-20 degrees up and down.

Appear Quantitative

According to researchers at Cornell, people are more likely to believe a claim if it 'looks and smells scientific'. Graphs and charts are as scientific as they get, so grab a whiteboard, draw X- and Y-axes liberally and then slap on dots, bars, columns, pies, etc. To up the scientific ante, throw in random statistics to justify your stand. A recent study conducted by Cambridge University showed that 76 per cent of professionals who worked in organizations with more than fifty employees, accepted facts stated by co-workers without the slightest of doubts. Now I made that up but didn't it sound believable?

People admire statistics so they need to be impressive, not necessarily correct: Seventy per cent of the Earth is water. Sixty per cent of a human body is water. So, on average, 65 per cent of the world must be water. You can also state obvious facts in a cool way: A summer without heat is winter. Or throw in cryptic one-liners and let people try to discern what exactly you are referring to: No one minds the smell of their own fart...

The Pareto Principle or the 80-20 rule essentially states that 80 per cent of outcomes are caused by 20 per cent of the causes or factors. 80 per cent of the world's wealth for example, is controlled by 20 per cent of its population; 80 per cent of crimes are committed by roughly 20 per cent of criminals, etc. You can also apply this rule blindly in discussions. 'I would estimate about 80 per cent of our complaints are coming from about 20 per cent of our customers,' 'I hazard a guess that the top 20 per cent of our products are pulling in about 80 per cent of the revenues.' And then sit back and wait till someone validates the numbers and looks at you in awe.

Finally, force people to think harder by quantifying your queries. 'On a scale of 1 to 10, what do you think of that new marketing campaign?' rather than, 'Hey dude, ad kaisa laga?'

Play Mind Games

By now, people will be sensing that you aren't contributing much; it's a good time to play some mind games.

Divert the group: Interrupt a discussion with, 'Excuse me, I just want to make three quick points here. A. I think we should..., B. we must do...' Rather than focusing on the content, people start counting the number of points you make. And by labelling them A, B, C. instead of 1, 2, 3, you have further muddled them as they are trying to correlate numbers to alphabets. You can talk gibberish for all you want—no one is focusing.

Pretend to read minds: Letting people believe that you can mind read makes you seem in control and they'll be more likely to listen to you. 'I know that you must be thinking that this proposal is really expensive. Let me tell you why you are wrong...'

Admit that your colleague is a know-it-all: To avoid objection from a colleague, admit that he is a know-it-all; look at your boss, point to your colleague and make your point in a matter-of-fact fashion. 'He knows better than I do that next quarter is going to tank completely.' Now it's very hard for someone to contradict you when you've admitted that he knows better. As he stands confused and processes what his reaction should be, move to the next point.

Speak just before your adversary: Whenever someone has to speak, he pays the least attention to the person speaking immediately prior as he is busy preparing (the next-in-line effect). If you have an adversary in the room, make your points immediately before it's his turn; you can even abuse him in your speech and he wouldn't notice.

Leverage your boss: If the boss makes such a bizarre inference that leaves the room stunned, immediately make eye contact with him and give him a silent nod—'That was truly visionary. The rest of these idiots don't get it but I do. Well done Sir, well done!'

If he is messaging anyone during the meeting, pull out your phone and start tapping keys. Look at him, smile, and get back to your pretend messaging. Let your colleagues believe that you have a private chat session on with the boss. There's no easier way to make them insecure.

Interrupt The Meeting

Finally, when you have absolutely nothing left to contribute, be an understated nuisance and distract your colleagues.

Do the 'meeting walk': Author-comedian Sarah Cooper has some useful hints on appearing smart in meetings including pacing around the room with your arms folded. You can do, what I call, the 'meeting walk'. Stand up halfway through a presentation, lean against a wall, and stare intently at the screen for a few minutes. Then, walk closer to the screen—completely ignoring the presenter—look closely at whatever's displayed, return to your spot against the wall and continue staring. After a while, return to your seat, open your pad, scribble some numbers and shut it. There will be a hush in the room as everyone tries to process what just happened.

Ask to go back a few slides: She also recommends interrupting the presenter and asking him to go back a slide.

In fact, ask him to go back a few and confuse him as he toggles with the 'Previous Slide' and 'Next Slide' buttons. 'No, not this, the earlier one. Go back one more. No next one ... Yes, that's it this one.' Stare at the slide for a few minutes as the room waits with bated breath for your spectacular inferences and then allow him to continue without any further elaboration. Let everyone wonder what it is that you have discovered but are keeping to yourself.

Grab a marker: When heated discussions aren't going anywhere, grab a marker, rush to the whiteboard and start scribbling anything. The chances are that you will be drowned out by all the voices and this little charade of yours will achieve nothing, so you can just screw back the marker cap in disgust and return to your seat. But you will come across as the mediator who tried to bring order to an otherwise senseless meeting.

Put the phone on vibrate near crockery: Put your phone on vibrate near any crockery on the conference table. It's as fascinating as it is annoying—watching water quiver and plates tremble every time you receive a call. Further kudos if you can make it appear that a colleague's phone is causing this disturbance.

Calculate the per minute cost of faffing: Estimate the total annual compensation of all attendees and divide it by 120,000, the approximate number of working minutes in a year. So, if it's a ten-person meeting with the CEO to a management trainee present and the total estimated annual compensation of the group is Rs 30 million, the per minute notional expense of everyone faffing is 30,000,000 / 120,000 = Rs 250. At frequent intervals announce what the tab has run up to. 'Rs 5,000 down already,' you can say twenty minutes into the meeting and keep up the scoring at intervals of Rs 2,500. All will appreciate your cost consciousness.

Every Meeting Needs a Nazar-Battu

The evil eye is a malicious glare from someone that turns out to be a curse for the person at the receiving end. Most cultures have created talismans or protective measures to ward off the evil eye. In the Middle East, they put up the hamsa hand—a hand with five outstretched fingers and a green or blue eye on the palm. In the Mediterranean, disks or balls with concentric blue circles are extremely popular. And closer home in India, people use a nazar-battu—a bracelet, charm, or object such as a lemon with seven chillies.

Sooner or later in meetings, your boss is going to vent his pent-up anger and frustration on someone; you just need to ensure that it isn't you. Your primary instinct is to avoid his evil eye and therefore all meetings need a nazar-battu. It doesn't matter how much the honcho hates you as long as he hates someone even more. So slouch back, stay silent and wait for the nazar-battu to open his mouth. Because invariably your boss will lose it at him and once he's down that path, you're secure. And in any event, always tie a lemon and chillies on your laptop as a backup measure.

Dialling in on Conference Calls

If you can wrangle permission to skip the meeting and dial in on a conference call instead, it makes things easier.

If people expect you to be on the road, intermittently play pre-recorded sounds such as street traffic or a plane taking off. You can even play the loud, urgent honk of a truck followed by screeching tires ... pause for a few seconds and then whisper into the phone, 'Phew, close call.'

Speak extremely fast and people won't catch your useless points but your participation will be registered. When asked difficult questions, blow into your phone—foo foo foo so that it appears that there's a lot of static. Intersperse your answer with more foo foos to keep up the charade. If a question takes you entirely by surprise, put the phone on mute, prepare your response, unmute and start your answer halfway through a sentence. You will be immediately interrupted with, 'We missed you there. Can you please repeat?' Pretend that your phone was inadvertently on mute and start over.

The last resort, if you find yourself completely in the soup, to pretend that you can't hear anything—just keep saying

'Hello, Hello' agitatedly as if you are genuinely concerned. And then disconnect the call—people will think that the call just dropped and by the time you log back on, the group would have moved to the next topic.

In Conclusion...

It's critical that you absorb and effectively implement the strategies in this chapter as early as you can. You don't need to learn by trial and error in your important meetings; wander around the office and gatecrash any random meeting that catches your fancy. Take a seat at the back, let people assume that you are from Finance or IT, enjoy the cookies sponsored by some other department, and test out some of these techniques. Even if you attend just one meeting daily over a forty-year career, that's over 10,000 meetings you will participate in. You will not find a bigger, better or more consistent canvas to display your mediocrity and please don't underestimate this opportunity.

HELPFUL BUSINESS JARGON

I recommend dropping in some business jargon and buzzwords in meetings to enhance the perception that you are trying to create. Here are some clichés that I find most relevant. To clarify, I am not reinventing the wheel but simply taking a stab at classifying the low hanging fruit. At the end of the day, you should leverage whatever you deem appropriate and do the needful.

Jargon that makes you appear intelligent:

- We can leverage this
- We need to think out of the box
- Let me do some quick back-of-the-envelope calculations
- This involves a lot of moving parts
- Let's not try and boil the ocean
- Let's peel the onion further
- My ballpark estimate is...
- That's a very cookie cutter approach
- We got to take this from soup to nuts
- We are talking an X per cent delta here...
- So, what is the value proposition here?
- I'm just thinking laterally here
- Let's blue sky a bit
- We are creating a body of work
- We don't want to be cannibalizing our product

Jargon to be regarded as a mature team player:

- Let's agree to disagree
- But what does our customer want?
- Let me call out the elephant in the room
- We seem to have all the ducks in a row
- What are we bringing to the table?
- Let's not keep moving the goal posts
- It is what it is...
- Just want to give you a heads up...
- Let's keep each other in the loop on this one
- It's a win-win situation

Jargon to be perceived as a go-getter:

- O This will move the needle
- O We can hit the ground running
- O It's low hanging fruit
- O Let's take it to the next level
- O We have a brief window of opportunity
- O This will give us the biggest bang for the buck
- O It's starting to gain traction
- O What are the best practices here?
- O We have a blue ocean opportunity in front of us
- O We need to build on our core competencies
- O Keep going until we have critical mass
- O We need to get out of fire-fighting mode

Jargon that demonstrates leadership qualities:

- O We need all hands on deck
- O Let's give this our 110 per cent
- O Let's not reinvent the wheel
- O This is where the rubber meets the road
- O You need to walk and chew gum
- O Let's not piss in the wind
- O I need a drop-dead date
- O We need a paradigm shift
- O Let's not put lipstick on a pig
- O We got to walk the talk

Jargon to help you procrastinate:

- I'll circle back to you
- I will run the numbers on it
- Let's go back to the drawing board
- Let's touch base in a bit. Ping me
- I don't have the bandwidth right now
- It's on my radar
- Let's put this on the back-burner
- I have too many balls in the air right now
- I have a lot on my plate
- I'll get back by close of play tomorrow
- I'll have to deep dive/drill down into this and get back
- I have a hard stop at X hours
- Let's park that for now
- It's in the pipeline

5

PROCRASTINATION: THE ART OF DOING NOTHING

Maintaining comfortable periods of limbo

Procrastination is the second leg of the Holy Trinity and you need to continually postpone until tomorrow what could have been done today. It's not easy to perfect the art of doing nothing; it's like meditating, only in a cubicle rather than some shala. But it must be done because procrastination helps you avoid success. Each success simply raises expectations and by delaying any task, you are merely keeping expectations of people around you at manageable levels. Which is a very good thing.

The Art of Doing Nothing

Most meetings, irrespective of how smoothly one navigates them, end up generating work—usually termed 'deliverables'. Some tyrannical bosses even anoint a specific professional to note down what was discussed and make a tracker of deliverables—an activity known as keeping minutes. This lackey then circulates these minutes and incessantly follows up for status updates. It's horrid.

WIP (Work in Progress) is an awesome acronym that immediately gives a veil of credence to whatever it is that you are not doing. Use it whenever the aforementioned flunky follows up and all will believe that a large team of motivated employees is on the ball, making all efforts to complete the project. There is a strange ambiguity to WIP—no finality, no details—just a hope that something will eventually be accomplished. And until then, it's a comfortable period of limbo during which you can dream up ways to delay things even further.

If various individuals or teams are given similar tasks, let the others dive into execution while you wait and watch. Keenly observe them brainstorm, flounder, make mistakes, and test various options before you even consider starting. You will get a good sense of what fails and can focus on implementing only whatever works. Sometimes it's not about who finishes first, it's about who finishes best. This is not even procrastination, it's more like a last mover advantage.

Finally, remember that work expands to fill any remaining time until the deadline, so take any output to your boss at the very last minute. Any earlier and he will make changes and have you redo stuff. So even if you are ready, hold on for as long as you can.

Procrastination for Managers

The amount of time that you can expect to work each day is correlated to your span of control—the number of direct reports that you have. You need to work approximately two hours per day for every direct report so if you have four directs, you can plan to put in eight hour days and if you have seven, you will be working 14-hour days. I advise an organizational structure where you have one, or a maximum of two directs, at any point in time.

The dangers of decisions

It takes tremendous skill to reach the Zen-like state where you are accomplishing absolutely nothing. Particularly since you don't want to draw too much attention to what you are up to. So, waffle on decisions, sleep over them, weigh pros and cons, put things on the back burner and keep going back to the drawing board—once things move, more work is created. Too much analysis leads to paralysis and all projects should face death by inaction under your watch.

If the project involves any calculations at all, ask for simulations, have all scenarios modelled out and push your team to cell XFD1048576, the ultimate depth of Excel, before you take any decision. As the model is being presented, challenge every assumption while furiously moving the cursor back and forth on the screen, 'This is wrong, change X to Y...' as your serfs try to keep track and take notes at the same time. End with, 'Go make all these changes and let's look at the revised model.' Repeat this process again and again.

Or simply answer 'Yes' when presented with some choices and unsure about what decision to take. So if your team asks if they should launch the marketing campaign this quarter or postpone it to next year, look at them as if you are deeply contemplating the issue. And then answer 'Yes' and walk away, leaving a confused silence behind.

The beauty of maintaining status quo

Whenever you require a decision from others, provide 'maintain status quo', which is simply an acceptable way of saying 'do nothing', as one of the possible courses of action.

Option 1 - An extremely expensive option
Option 2 - An extremely complex option
Option 3 - An extremely time-consuming option
Option 4 - Maintain status quo
Option 5 - An extremely illogical option
Option 6 - An extremely ambiguous option

The boss will usually reject expensive option 1 outright and the Einstein in the room will immediately point out why option 5 is nonsensical. People tend to avoid options where there is missing information and unknown outcomes and option 6 will automatically be rejected. A healthy debate will ensue on option 2 and keep stirring the pot by highlighting all the complexities around it. A heated discussion will also take place on Option 3 and with feigned impatience, reiterate the long timelines envisioned. Eventually, the group will tire and turn towards the last remaining option 4—maintain status quo. Keep a straight face as someone suggests that waiting and watching is probably the best course of action for now, more heads will nod and the boss will wrap up in agreement and call for a follow-up meeting a few weeks later. Your objective of uniting everyone into doing nothing is successful.

Decision-making in teams

It's also useful to understand how decisions are made in team environments. This is rarely a smooth journey and leaves most people frustrated. The process depends on the composition of the team. A team comprising of early careers take decisions by consensus. No one has enough experience to hold strong views on anything and invariably all opinions are heard before the group reaches an acceptable agreement. Teams of middle managers, with their jostling and politicking, are unable to achieve this level of collaboration and take a decision by majority vote. After hours of brainstorming, the group breaks into camps and then like school kids, they go around voting to determine which option has more backers. Lastly, a senior leadership team doesn't even exhibit such cordiality. Meetings invariably break down in a cesspool of one-upmanship and the decision is finally taken by the topmost designation in the room.

Other useful tricks

Commute to work using public transport as you will arrive tired and harried and your boss will sympathize at the inordinate effort you're making, simply to show up. You can justify excessive coffee and bathroom breaks without him batting an eyelid. He will hesitate to call you in early or stay back late and your work–life balance will be dramatically better than those Ubering it in.

If you are getting bored as you procrastinate, a good way to kill time is playing a round of 'Who wants to be a rumour monger?' Call a colleague and start the conversation with a surreptitious, 'Hey, have you heard—this is serious shit...' and insert a rumour—the sales head is moving to a competitor, someone is sleeping with someone, there are expense pressures and lay-offs are coming. End with a

'Please don't tell this to anyone!' and hang up. Then sit back and measure how long it takes for this rumour to get back to you with your phone ringing and some other colleague at the other end, 'Hey, have you heard—this is serious shit...'

Finally, your phone battery is a very useful accessory that lets you measure the effectiveness of procrastination. At the end of the day, if your battery is at more than 50 per cent, you have obviously been working hard. If it's close to drained or better yet, had to be recharged during the day, good job—you achieved a fantastic level of dilly-dallying.

Appearing Busy

Just because you are procrastinating doesn't mean that you cannot appear busy. Busy people are perceived as achievers and the following shenanigans will help create the impression of you being an overworked yet in-control multitasker.

Alt-tab the day: Put a screenshot of a complicated looking spreadsheet as your wallpaper so that anyone glancing at your idle screen will be fooled into thinking you're analyzing a complex file. And keep multiple windows open on your monitor and toggle frantically between them. Alt-Tab, Alt-Tab, Alt-Tab.

Use sound recordings: Record and play the sound of a pounding keyboard on loop at your desk. You can be taking a nap but to the casual passer-by, you are working furiously. When you have company, keep clicking your pen. Click. Click. Click. Click. Click. Click. You'll look busy. Pretend that you're trying to remember a password as you click and you will look even busier.

Invest heavily in scribbling: Your desk should be messy enough for people to think you're swamped but clean enough to quickly locate whatever your supervisor needs. You need to look occupied not disorganized. Scatter business cards of random people around the cubicle and stick lots of post-it notes, in varied colours, on the walls. Scribble important imaginary tasks on all of them—stay in touch for new business, execute Project X, disable nuclear warheads.

Walk, print and tap: Writer Tamara Jenkins advises to always walk around the office with a sense of urgency. Take out ten minutes to do the office walkathon. Grab a bunch of files, shove them under your armpit and take a long, circuitous and hurried route around the floor, looking extremely focused. Take a brief pause at the printer and wait, tapping your feet impatiently. Shake your head as nothing obviously appears and walk briskly back to your desk. Repeat every two hours.

Grandstand effectively: Have a friend call you and carry on an imaginary work conversation with him. Discuss hypothetical strategies, a plan of action, end with, 'I will get started on this immediately, Sir,' and hang up with gusto. Mutter, 'Damn, another tight deadline project from the boss,' loud enough for your colleagues to hear.

If it is your boss who walks in while you are on the phone with anyone, raise your voice and say all the things that will impress him, 'I understand what you are saying but we have to do what is good for the customer.' You may be talking to your mother-in-law for all we know. But he doesn't.

Have a list of imaginary projects: How do you usually respond when someone casually asks, 'What's going on?' Most people reply with a cursory, 'Not much,' 'All good,' or the colloquial 'Phatti hui hai.' Don't be most people and instead spout out an exhaustive list of imaginary projects and tight deadlines. End with a tired sigh, 'What about you?'

Schedule these fictitious projects and meetings and always maintain a full calendar by creating dummy meetings to fill in all gaps. Whenever people access it, they should see your diary chock-a-block full.

You decide your compensation

Let's say your monthly compensation is Rs 100,000 but you spend only half the day working and the other half procrastinating. Your effective salary is therefore Rs 200,000 as that's what the organization will pay you over two months to do what an efficient employee would do in one. So, when comparing salaries, don't look at absolute figures as they're misleading; consider effective salaries and I'm sure you'll be at the top of the totem pole.

The organization decides what to pay you but you choose how much you'll work. If you aren't happy with the compensation, simply procrastinate some more.

Take some time to recharge

Intersperse long bouts of procrastination with spurts of intense hard work. The best time to display your most productive and efficient self is Friday afternoon when other colleagues are winding down. You won't need to do much to stand out as the busiest bee in the comb and it's a short pretence anyway—in a few hours, it will be time to leave.

Finally, constant procrastination is tiring and occasionally call in sick so that you can recover at home and return to work to procrastinate with a renewed energy. And lounging in the comfort of your bedroom is infinitely better than in your cubicle. When making the call, lie down on the bed, hang your head from the side and then dial your boss—you will sound extremely congested and he will quickly end the call with a concerned 'Take care'.

In Conclusion...

The corporate world always makes a huge hullaballoo about meeting deadlines and being efficient and productive but there isn't much benefit to it. Postponing things to a later date gives you, and everyone else, something to look forward to and hope is a wonderful thing. Procrastination is not a weakness—it is an outcome of your strong desire to do things so perfectly that you'd rather not start something than do it poorly. An understanding boss will appreciate this.

The *Bhagavad Gita* wisely says, there is action in inaction and inaction in action. So, do not be in a rush to whittle down your to-do list or be a go-getter. I'm sure you will eventually get down to completing whatever you have to—by Monday, Tuesday, Wednesday, Thursday, Friday, Saturday, Sunday or Someday.

6

CYA: COVER YOUR ASS

Avoiding the shit when it hits the fan

If you are remotely involved in any sort of work, you will sooner or later have to conduct some CYA (Cover your Ass). This final leg in the Holy Trinity, is the act of anticipating and taking precautions for all situations where things could go badly due to your incompetence or negligence. And when they do, others should have nothing to blame you for. Never be the last moron standing in the corporate game of musical chairs.

CYA doesn't require a lot of special preparation, just some basic common sense.

Don't take on doomed projects: Some projects are doomed to fail and even before they start, one knows that they won't go anywhere. The only question is who will be the fall guy when the project team is done sinking the Titanic. If you get a whiff of a doomed project near your cubicle, stay far away from it.

Don't sign off on anything: Do not sign off on any memos or legal documents and dilly-dally until they disappear or your boss or junior is forced to sign them. When things go wrong, the first question that authorities ask is, 'Who all approved the damn memo?' and you don't want your name popping up. If you are cornered into signing stuff, use a variety of different signatures and inks on the document. That way when you are standing in the witness box with the prospect of *tazirat-e-Hind dafa teen-sau-do* dangling over your head, you can look suitably confused and innocent.

Blame technology: The problem with passing the buck on to humans is that they can deny any wrongdoing and clarify their position. It's far easier to fault technology, systems or software for any goof-ups. 'I had completed the report but the systems crashed and I had to start all over again.' 'I don't know how these numbers are wrong—there must be some software issue and I will have it rechecked.' What's your boss going to do—go the server room and ask the metal boxes if they messed up?

Blame the environment: Whenever things go particularly bad, obfuscate the issue by blaming the business environment. Either it was bad—'We are coming out from a terrible recession', it is bad—'We are in a grim business climate' or will be bad—'We are heading for miserable times'. If that doesn't work, accept defeat and say that everyone is responsible— you, the entire team, function, and even the organization is to blame. When you claim that everyone is responsible, the eventual outcome is that no one is held responsible.

Make your KRAs (Key Result Areas) a shared goal: Whether accountable for delivering a sales target or ensuring a process within turnaround times, an excellent way to CYA is to make any responsibility a shared goal.

Are you responsible for selling insurance policies? Rope in the marketing team—'I need 5,000 leads from marketing this month if I am to achieve my sales target' Loop in Operations—'I need 99.9 per cent efficiency in booking my sales, else negative customer feedback will impact further sales. Lasso in HR—I need to hire 50 new agents to meet my goals.' Then hard code all these lead, process and recruitment targets as critical variables to achieve success.

The more departments that you can snare, the murkier your individual responsibilities become. When you fail, no one will know who to blame and by the time your boss unravels the interdependencies, you will have moved on to the next project.

Seek a legal opinion: You can put a spanner in the works of any work and protect yourself by seeking a legal opinion. A legal opinion by definition is the opinion of a lawyer. Lawyers by profession opine on the law. The law in general can be interpreted in many ways with appropriate caveats and fine print. A legal opinion therefore is a highly ambiguous document that resolves little and raises more questions than it addresses. If you are stuck or merely want to buy some time, ask for a legal opinion on the various possible courses of action. Then sit back and relax as lawyers prepare an expensive, confusing report that leaves no one any wiser.

Ration CYA Judiciously

CYA is not required for all messes, so ration it judiciously. Keep small problems hush-hush as they usually get fixed on their own and disappear. There's no point in making a hue and cry because even if discovered, they will at best draw a rap on the knuckle.

Big issues can get you strung up and the best way to CYA is to make them even bigger and therefore everyone's problem. So, make it as disturbing as possible and delegate upward, sharing all gory details with your boss and anyone remotely relevant. Don't be the only one losing sleep and let everyone toss and turn till it blows over, or blows up, completely.

Another benefit of spreading the pain is that the shit of big problems first hits the fan on the boardroom ceiling. If the management team is knee deep in poop, dealing with lawsuits, regulators, government officials, fines, etc., you will invariably be forgotten. And when the sacrificial scapegoat is required, the embroilment of senior people betters your chances of slipping out scot-free.

Finally, the most proactive way of CYA-ing humungous problems is to blow the whistle on them. Bring them to the attention of top management as an observer or victim rather than the creator of the disaster. This is guaranteed to throw the organization into a tizzy as also grant you immunity from any consequences. People have made careers by blowing the whistle on problems of their own creation and while the organization struggles to deal with them, they get transferred out to lucrative postings, ostensibly to protect them from retribution. What could be better?

In Conclusion...

You probably remember the old arcade game where one had to direct a bunch of frogs across a busy screen. Each frog would start at the bottom and dodge fast-moving vehicles, jump onto logs and escape alligators to make it safely to the other side. In the corporate world, you are the frog, and all those obstacles are work. Work will keep attacking you with varying speeds, from all directions, and your sole responsibility is to evade it. Jump up, dive down, skip left, hop right—do what it takes to sidestep it and survive for as long as you can.

But invariably, there will be the time when work succeeds in colliding with you. Boom—Crash—Bang—the screen shakes! It's alright. Be ready with your explanations as to what happened. Blame the crash on the previous frog who wasn't fast enough. Or the next one who was asking too many questions. Or the damned alligator who appeared out of nowhere. Or the log which was very slippery. It just wasn't your fault. And then wait for a few moments until 'Next Life' flashes. Because if you CYA properly, that's what you will keep getting in the workplace.

FEEL GOOD ANECDOTES

Since the clothes bared all, the CEO covered

Lululemon is a premium women's clothing brand that established itself by selling overpriced yoga wear. But women swore by it, making it one of the most successful global apparel companies. Until they launched a batch of their signature yoga pants that just happened to be too sheer. They were virtually transparent when exposed to the twisty contorting moves that they were put through in yoga studios and this, while plausibly exciting to the men in the room, was not very suitable for the wearers. And when women took the pants back to stores, they were very politely told to put them on and bend over so staff could verify how see-through they were.

Now, like any reasonable consumer-oriented company, and even more so when you are causing your customers to be almost naked in public, Lululemon could have just withdrawn and replaced these yoga pants. But the management decided to take a slightly more unconventional and literal route to CYA and accused the customers instead. Founder-Chairman Chip Wilson appeared in a televised interview and blamed the effect on fat customers who he claimed ruined the pants by rubbing their thighs together. As he mentioned, 'Quite frankly, some women's bodies just actually don't work for Lululemon's yoga pants. It's about the rubbing through the thighs and how much pressure is there.'

It required some serious pranayama to deal with the backlash that followed.

Without a shred of doubt

A robust document shredder is a necessary accessory for most CYA activities. Enron, a US-based energy company, had a spectacular run when it crossed over $100 billion in revenue in 2000 and was named America's Most Innovative Company by the venerated *Fortune* magazine for six years in a row. Its most significant innovation, unknown to most people at that time, was in its accounting standards with assets, revenues and profits being grossly overstated. Helping in this endeavour to create the world's biggest audit disaster was the Big Five accounting firm of Arthur Andersen. Enron cooked books, Arthur Andersen certified them, and collected over $50 million a year in audit and consulting fees.

The gig had to give though and authorities started investigating Enron in 2001. Fearing that the noose would also tighten around their neck, Arthur Andersen took the honourable route out and decided to shred any incriminating documents they had related to their client. They first outsourced the shredding to an external company but soon, given the volume and sensitivity, moved it in-house. So, they borrowed a big ass shredder from Enron, created a 'shred room' and put people on the job. In all, they destroyed an estimated one ton of documents.

This brave attempt at CYA notwithstanding, their sins came to light and the eighty-nine-year-old-firm, like their client, went bankrupt. Eighty-five thousand people lost their jobs and the shredder was hopefully returned to Enron.

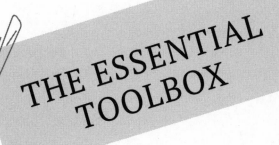

THE ESSENTIAL TOOLBOX

7

TO CC: OR NOT TO BCC:

Writing confusing emails

Success is 1 per cent inspiration, 2 per cent perspiration and 97 per cent communication. How you exchange, muddle or withhold information plays a crucial role in how well you do professionally. We have explored body language, verbal and telephonic communication techniques and shall now delve into email communication and presentation skills. We will then apply these learnings in the context of a common situation—getting reviewed by the boss.

Email is a ubiquitous part of corporate life. People nowadays rarely use the phone, walk into colleague's cabins or converse in corridors, instead preferring to express their views on a screen and hitting 'Send'. The most significant benefit of email is that it is one way—you can comment without having to deal with immediate reactions. And you can take your time in reverting to whatever response you get via email. Email is simply delayed conversation.

It does have its shortcomings. Imagine that you are arguing with your spouse and make a very valid point. However, she suddenly quotes a contradictory statement that you made fifteen years ago. You are stumped by her ability to pull out relevant nuggets from so far back and raise your hands in defeat. That's essentially what email communication is—a trail for posterity that will never be entirely wiped out. Treat it as you would a conversation with your partner—with great thought, care and dread.

Communicating with the Boss

It's straightforward to deal with emails from your boss. Simply set up an auto reply 'Okay!' and it saves you a lot of trouble with reading and typing. Some bosses happen to be incessant dunners who inundate employees with emails at all hours—reminders, follow ups, copying one on irrelevant messages and so on. In such cases, you may want to politely check with his assistant if there is an option to unsubscribe from his list.

When you initiate communication with your boss, it's slightly more complicated. The mode of contact depends on the outcome you want from the conversation. If you are merely updating him and no action is required, use the phone; such chats are crisp and perfectly at the cusp of formality and casualness. If it's important and you need an immediate decision, have a face-to-face meeting—barge into his office, explain the situation and demand instant resolution. The complicated cases are those where a decision is required but you'd rather that he not take one—things are going along smoothly and any action will just create additional work and complexity. Vague email communication, where he doesn't even get a hint of what is needed, is ideal.

Start your email with an innocuous subject heading that doesn't give anything away—this simple universal phrase works marvellously.

Re: Hello

Address him with an inane salutation that elicits a groan even before the first paragraph is read.

Dear Boss,
  Greetings of the day!!!

Then provide a lengthy introduction of small talk.

It has been a while since my last email to you and I hope this finds you in the pinky of health. It is cold here in the basement, Brrrr, but I trust the weather in your top floor corner office is warmer. I hope bhabhiji and kids are keeping well—they must be growing wide and up so fast.

Move on to your professional life, barely making a brief allusion to the decision that needs to be made. Throw him off with vague adjectives and adverbs and random intermittent usage of **boldface**, <u>underlining</u> and *italics*.

All of us here in the basement are doing well. Jignesh bhai got promoted and is moving up to the first floor next month. Rupal ben made a ***<u>killing</u>*** in day trading and has submitted her resignation. The rest of us are busy with our projects. Finance is working on the next plan cycle and the sales team on field calls. I am<u> extremely </u>

<u>swamped</u> as well, slightly behind schedule but burning the midnight oil, on the productivity enhancement project—it has been interesting and I am learning a lot. It's quite like going back to my college days when I was learning **computer engineering** and I discovered that by upgrading the software on my home PC, my productivity would improve and I am now led to think, in my infinite wisdom and the <u>guidance of seniors</u> like yourself, that the same can happen at work if we were to do so with your kind blessings. I am going to the gym daily and god willing, by the next appraisal cycle I shall have at least one of my targeted **six packs**.

Conclude by summarizing the mail and make a random new point to muddle him further.

So to conclude, all is well on the professional front here in the basement and the project is moving along at a peppy pace. Our servers have crashed and we will be offline for the next month. My focus on fitness continues to remain strong.

End by fuzzily putting the ball in his court.

It is always a source of great joy to hear from you, Sir, and my eyes will lie outstretched in front of my screen awaiting your prestigious revert.

Humbly yours,
Rishi

As the coup-de-grace of ambiguity, post script with a

PS—Attachment enclosed

However, 'forget' to enclose the attachment and instead send it subsequently in a new email with a different subject heading. He won't have the mails and attachments grouped in one place and consequently, will end up ignoring everything.

Re: Apologies
Dear Boss,
   Greetings of the day and a thousand apologies!!! I forgot to attach the attachment to my last mail. Here it is attached.

Forgetfully yours,
Rishi

PS—Attachment enclosed

Now in the communication above, you have very effectively shared your recommendation on the productivity enhancement project—the software needs to be upgraded for the entire team— and have sought his approval to do so. But it's very likely that he completely missed it and won't even revert to this mail, let alone approve anything. So you can chillabrate till he eventually follows up on the project, at which point let him know that it's stuck at his end, awaiting approval. And show him this trail as proof.

Email Communication with Colleagues

You can use email effectively to gain the upper hand on colleagues and keep them leaning insecurely on their back foot.

Respond at your own pace: Keep them edgy and irritable by not responding to emails until they have followed up a few times and wasted valuable time chasing you. Set the expectations clearly—you will read and hit reply only when you want to. Not just email, if you absent-mindedly answer the phone when they call, pretend that you are the voice mail, 'Hi, you have reached Rishi's voicemail. Please leave a message. Beep.' And forget about it.

Annoy them with Read Receipts: When you do respond, ensure that you request a read receipt. Essentially, as soon as they open your mail, a pop up box will ask them to confirm that they have read it; extremely annoying.

Schedule delivery of mails at late night: Most email programs allow you to schedule the delivery of your messages to a time of your choosing and rather than send them as you draft them, delay some to post midnight. Your boss and colleagues will get your emails at ungodly hours and will be extremely impressed with the effort you are putting.

Use Out of Office effectively: Use the Out of Office feature to further impress people. Whenever you are away turn it on, keeping it vaguely honest— 'I am travelling with limited access to mail...' Don't specify whether you are on holiday or work and include as many people as possible in your auto-reply message. 'Contact X for Project A, Y for Project B, Z for Project C.' This makes you look extraordinarily busy and motivates whoever has been listed as a temporary in charge.

Include a signature: Use your email's signature block to promote yourself. Emails circulate and the more people who read your publicity material, the better it is for your career. Include as much awe-inspiring information as you can in your signature.

Rishi Piparaiya
Absolutely Stunning Manager—the best in this corporation.
Awarded a certificate of participation in an art competition in middle school

Send joint emails from your drop: Sometimes important organization-wide announcements or memos need to be jointly signed by more than one manager. An employee is moving from Unit A to Unit B for example and the announcement will therefore be signed by both the unit-heads. Irrespective of who all sign an announcement, make sure it is released from your email ID—whoever sends a joint email is essentially higher in the pecking order.

Make colleagues insecure: Imagine standing in a large group and you lean over and whisper to the person next to you. You then walk around and whisper to each person in the group except one colleague, ignoring him completely. Won't he feel isolated and insecure, wondering why he has been left out? The email equivalent is sending a group mail but not copying someone who should have been. He will invariably learn about it and become profoundly insecure. Which is the sole purpose of your life.

CC:, BCC: or FWD: FYI?

One of the first things most people do on receiving an email is check who all have been copied. Having a senior executive on the mail trail puts them on attention and influences the nature as well as the speed of their response. You can use this to your advantage. Your options when you send emails are to transparently copy a senior executive ('Cc:'), surreptitiously blind copy him/her ('Bcc:') or go for the ultimate slime manoeuvre and send the mail to your colleague and then forward it one-on-one to the boss ('Fwd: FYI'). The flowchart will help you decide which course of action to take.

You should 'Reply All' on messages frequently—if your boss sends an article to the entire team to read, reply all with a 'Thank you, this should be wonderful.' If HR sends a message to the complete country list announcing an unscheduled holiday, reply all with a 'Damn!' While Reply All overloads mailboxes and creates inefficiencies for everyone, it gets you noticed.

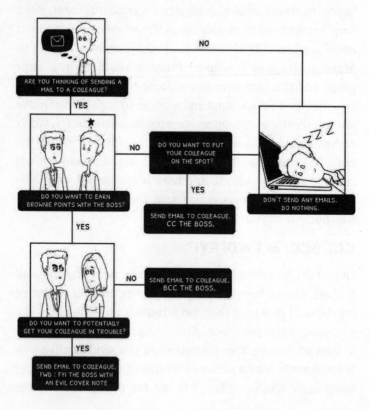

Lastly, use the FYI/A (For your Information and Action) liberally with your juniors. There's no need to explain what needs to be done, why and by when; it's a simple delegation of work and FYI/A is an absolute delight for shirkers. You can also use it in other positive ways; occasionally, you might be lucky enough to receive a confidential message from a government minister in Africa who needs your help to smuggle funds out of the country. Pass on this lucrative opportunity to your boss—'Sir, FYI/A'. He will be most appreciative.

In Conclusion...

In organizations worldwide, email has emerged as a preferred form of business communication. While most people unassumingly see it purely as a fast and straightforward means of getting messages across, you now know better. Before you next hit 'Send', take a minute to pause and introspect. Can that innocuous message staring back at you help you avoid work, protect you from liabilities, strengthen your turf or incriminate a colleague? If not, you may want to reword it.

 FEEL GOOD ANECDOTES

Most of us have at some point, received a stinker from the boss. He's mad as heck and sends a raving ranting email, which makes you really low ☹.

Cheer up! It couldn't even come close to this zinger from Rebecca, a leader of the Delta Gamma sorority at the University of Maryland. She was extremely upset that the 'sisters' (members of her female social organization) were not being fun and social enough with fraternity brothers at Sigma Nu (the members of a counterpart male social organization). She sent an expletive and CAPS ridden tirade to the entire sorority imploring them to party harder and not be so boring. Resisting my urge to censor her language, I'm reproducing some of the extracts. She starts with an attention-grabbing opening:

> If you just opened this like I told you to, tie yourself down to whatever chair you're sitting in, because this email is going to be a rough fucking ride.

and comes straight to the point:

> For those of you that have your heads stuck under rocks, which apparently is the majority of this chapter, we have been FUCKING UP in terms of night time events and general social interactions with Sigma Nu. I've been getting texts on texts about people LITERALLY being so fucking AWKWARD and so fucking BORING. If you're reading this right now and saying to yourself 'But oh em gee Rebecca, I've been having so much fun with my sisters this week!' then punch yourself in the face right now so that I don't have to fucking find you on campus to do it myself.

Her authority is evident to anyone who even studied English as a third language.

> I do not give a flying eff, and Sigma Nu does not give a flying eff, about how much you fucking love to talk to your sisters. You have 361 days out of the fucking year to talk to sisters, and this week is NOT, I fucking repeat NOT ONE

OF THEM … Newsflash you stupid cocks: FRATS DON'T LIKE BORING SORORITIES. Oh wait, DOUBLE FUCKING NEWSFLASH: SIGMA NU IS NOT GOING TO WANT TO HANG OUT WITH US IF WE FUCKING SUCK, which by the way in case you're an idiot and need it spelled out for you, WE FUCKING SUCK SO FAR.

She thankfully seems to have some interest in the mental health of her wards.

Are you people fucking retarded?

Or well, maybe not.

That's not a rhetorical question, I LITERALLY want you to email me back telling me if you're mentally slow so I can make sure you don't go to anymore night time events.

She's remarkably in tune with her sisters' thoughts as they read her rant.

'But Rebecca!' you say in a whiny little bitch voice to your computer screen as you read this email, 'I've been cheering on our teams at all the sports, doesn't that count for something?' NO YOU STUPID FUCKING ASS HATS, IT FUCKING DOESN'T.

Sportsmanship is certainly not a virtue she values as she instructs who they should be cheering for at games.

I've gotten texts about people actually cheering for the opposing team. The opposing. Fucking. Team. ARE

YOU FUCKING STUPID?!! I don't give a SHIT about sportsmanship, YOU CHEER FOR OUR GODDAMN TEAM AND NOT THE OTHER ONE, HAVE YOU NEVER BEEN TO A SPORTS GAME? ARE YOU FUCKING BLIND? Or are you just so fucking dense ... I will fucking cunt punt the next person I hear about doing something like that, and I don't give a eff if you SOR me, I WILL FUCKING ASSAULT YOU.

For a minute, it seems that she has a tinge of regret, but not really.

'Ohhh Rebecca, I'm now crying because your email has made me oh so so sad.' Well good. If this email applies to you in any way, meaning if you are a little asswipe that stands in the corners at night or if you're a weird shit that does weird shit during the day, this following message is for you: DO NOT GO TO TONIGHT'S EVENT.

I'm not fucking kidding. Don't go ... I would rather have 40 girls that are fun, talk to boys, and not fucking awkward than 80 that are fucking faggots ... don't fucking show up unless you're going to stop being a goddamn cock block for our chapter. Seriously. I swear to fucking God if I see anyone being a goddamn boner at tonight's event, I will tell you to leave even if you're sober. I'm not even kidding. Try me.

And if anyone expected her to calm her farm towards the end, they'll be disappointed.

And for those of you who are offended at this email, I would apologize but I really don't give a fuck. Go fuck yourself.

(You can read the entire email by searching for 'Delta gamma freak out email.' And then you can thank your lucky stars that your boss is not a former sorority leader named Rebecca.)

8

THE POWER OF MAKING POINTS

Weaving stories on slides

As you stagnate up your career, you will find yourself increasingly focusing on a seemingly useless but critical activity—making presentations. You will spend days and nights working on slides and charts trying to put together a plausible tale that explains your shortcomings. Corporate life is all about weaving stories and the more fantastic the yarn, the more likely it is that you will taste success. It doesn't matter how good or bad your story is—it all boils down to how you present it. Here are some insights on stringing together fables that would make Aesop proud.

Leave the Audience Unprepared

Making a presentation is war, the audience your enemy and guerrilla warfare your strategy. Ambush them and take them completely by surprise—they should never know what's about to come and how hard it will hit them.

No pre-reads or handouts: Retain the element of surprise in all aspects for as long as you can. Never circulate any advance reading material as that will help your boss and audience come prepared. Don't even share the agenda and spring it up at the last possible minute. Likewise, don't give handouts that people can refer to while you are presenting. Postpone sharing all material until after the meeting is over and even then, make it as untidy and disorganized as possible. Handouts should be printed in black and white, double-sided, six slides to a page and stained with oil and haldi (turmeric), making them virtually unreadable.

Don't put an index sheet: Never give a framework or structure to a story that you are hell-bent on muddling. Dive straight into Slide 1 and keep going until you reach the final 'Thank You' slide. The audience should never know what'll come next; if they can't anticipate your slides, you don't need to anticipate their questions.

Page numbers are an information overload: Don't add page numbers to any presentation; they provide unnecessary information that can only backfire. 'Rishi, can you go back to Page 46 and explain the financials again,' is a specific instruction that you need to comply with. Contrast this to, 'Rishi, can you go back a few slides to that table and explain the financials,'—you can muck around, act confused and take your time finding the slide by which time the irritated questioner would have lost his train of thought.

Hide the Sunny Leone clips: The gathering will be scrutinizing your desktop as you set up your presentation while the projector is on. Incriminating files such as CVforHeadhunter.doc or BestofSunnyLeone.mov shouldn't be prominently displayed on your desktop. Also, turn off all notifications so flirty chat messages don't keep popping up while you present.

While on file names, people don't really give this attention and end up giving their documents asinine and meaningless names—Rishireport.doc, financefile.xls or julyppt.ppt. Impress people with intelligent labelling such as IndustrySWOT.doc, BudgetScenarios.xls, ConfidentialBoardStrategy.ppt, etc. It's unlikely that your content will awe them so at least the file name should.

Keep the Audience Distracted

Use all means to keep your audience side-tracked so their focus is on your ancillary moves, rather than the main presentation.

Grab sleepy slots: Grab speaking slots when the group will be most drowsy and disinterested, immediately after lunch, for example, or just before breaks when people are impatient to leave. Start your presentation in as monotonous a tone as manageable and you should see eyelids quickly droop.

Keep it busy: It's human nature to race ahead and read whatever's on the screen, even before you start speaking, so squeeze in as many bullets as you can on each slide. People will be engrossed trying to read ahead and you can mumble-jumble away. Follow the 10/20/30 rule for maximum distraction—size 10 font, 20 seconds per slide, 30 bullets on each slide.

Throw in confusing acronyms: Insert various acronyms— NPV, PSC, ROFLMAO, WTF, etc., without explanation. If people seek clarifications, look at them dismissively as if you expected better and move on to the next slide without answering.

The animation should make Disney proud: Presentation software comes with a multitude of eye-popping animation options and use them liberally. Text flying in from all directions, images crashing in, charts magically spiralling around—ensure that your presentation is a medley of as much animation as you can fit in. Have at least one bullet slowly text crawl, letter by letter, from the bottom of the page to its eventual resting place at the top; viewers should be pulling nails by the time it's finally formed.

And shoot for a Grammy with sound: Suddenly jolt the audience awake with sound effects; nothing like a foghorn resounding through the room just before you launch into a monologue on the impact of rising interest rates on the balance sheet.

Point the laser aimlessly: Keep flashing a laser pointer, the pen-like device that shines a red light, on the screen. While people are confusedly trying to figure out, like cats in viral videos, what exactly you are pointing at, move on to the next slide.

Experiment with communication styles: Gesticulate wildly as you talk and make slicing your throat actions with your fingers. Stare at a spot on your boss's nose as you speak to him—he will spend the rest of the meeting scratching his nostril. Frequently change your tone of voice—soft whispers to loud shrieks to threatening baritones. Keep experimenting.

Throw in a systems diagram: Insert a systems diagram, usually found in technical papers, in the middle of your presentation. It's a complicated amalgamation of shapes and lines that purportedly show how systems, databases, etc., are set up and is an instant turn-off to anyone other than computer geeks. It doesn't matter what you are presenting—

anything can be converted into a complicated process flow chart if you draw enough triangles, squares, cylinders and arrows.

Most people take a bathroom break or catch up on their emails when such slides come up. Therefore, insert it at a strategic point of your presentation, just before you are breaking bad news. The audience will switch off and you can gloss over your message. The only people listening in rapt attention would be the IT folk but they are irrelevant participants in corporate presentations anyway.

Smartly Made Charts and Tables are Your Strongest Allies

Irrespective of how bad your results are, use charts and tables wisely to appear a superstar.

Play with scales and arrows: No number looks bad relative to another number if the appropriate scale is used. Have sales fallen 20 per cent from 8,000 widgets to 6,400 widgets? Show it on a scale of 6,000 to 8,000 and you may as well attach your resignation as an annexure. But show it on a slightly more liberal scale (0 to 500,000) and the chances are that no one will notice.

Disorient with legends: A confusing legend is a key support and never put data labels on the chart; instead, place a legend as far from the chart as possible. To make it even harder to distinguish data, make charts in shades of grey rather than colours.

Plant errors: Highlight irrelevant numbers so that the key ones you want masked are overlooked. There's only a limited amount of feedback that people can give before they tire out, so plant a couple of basic errors—wrong spellings, incorrect use of grammar, addition mistakes in your presentation. The audience will expend their energy in pointing out all those easily fixable issues and not have attention to delve into the matters of real consequence.

In Conclusion...

As the adage goes, 'It's not what you say, but how you say it.' A presentation can be your best friend or your worst enemy, depending on how you approach it. It requires tremendous preparation and you can't just wing a lousy story, so be prepared to put in this effort. You have painstakingly spent so much time getting matters this screwed up and you can surely invest a little more in giving it a positive spin. You owe it to your ineptitude.

 FEEL GOOD ANECDOTES

You should supplement your confusing slides by speaking in absolute gibberish and making pronouncements that leave the smartest people scratching their heads. Here are some real-life examples to help you get started.

'I think that gay marriage should be between a man and a woman.'

– Arnold Schwarzenegger, Actor and politician

'Reports that say that something hasn't happened are always interesting to me, because as we know, there are known knowns; there are things we know we know. We also know there are known unknowns; that is to say we know there are some things we do not know. But there are also unknown unknowns—the ones we don't know we don't know.'

> – Donald Rumsfeld, Former Secretary of Defence, USA

'For those of you watching in black and white, Spurs are playing in yellow.'

> – John Motson, Football commentator

'Total spending will continue to rise and it will be a 0 per cent rise in 2013-14.'

> – Gordon Brown, Former British Prime Minister

'It depends upon what the meaning of the word "is" is. 'If 'is' means 'is and never has been' that's one thing—if it means 'there is none', that was a completely true statement.'

> - Bill Clinton, Former U.S. President, during his 1998 Grand Jury testimony about Monica Lewinsky

'I know what I believe. I will continue to articulate what I believe and what I believe—I believe what I believe is right.'

> – George W. Bush, Former U.S. President

'One word sums up probably the responsibility of any vice president, and that one word is "to be prepared".'

> – Dan Quayle, Former U.S. Vice President

'I could not fail to disagree with you less.'

> – Boris Johnson, British politician

'This morning I got up at night, 4 o'clock in the morning.'

> – Rahul Gandhi, Indian politician

9

LET'S TAKE IT OFFLINE

*Asking the right questions and answering
the wrong ones*

Communication at the workplace doesn't happen in statements but as a series of questions and answers. Your bosses and colleagues will ask you questions, which you will attempt to deflect or answer with questions of your own. They will follow up with additional questions and you will again try to side-track and this back and forth will continue. As Nobel Laureate Naguib Mahfouz wrote, 'You can tell whether a man is clever by his answers. You can tell whether a man is wise by his questions,' and I will coach you on how to appear both.

Giving Answers

The best way to appear clever with your answers is by avoiding giving any responses altogether. You shouldn't risk putting your foot in that mouth and being unable to extract it with a roomful of colleagues and seniors watching you. Ideally, do not answer any questions or elegantly mumbo-jumbo your way out of them, adopting the following strategies.

Time your bathroom breaks

Top professionals time their bathroom breaks to perfection and you should go, not when you have the urge to, but when it is most advantageous. Flip through the presentation, anticipate when you might be asked tough questions and a few slides prior, excuse yourself. Choose an appropriate moment; if you are from HR, step out when the sales guy is presenting as no one will give it a second thought. Then, when the high attrition numbers pop up a few minutes later, you will be in the restroom leaning on the flush. The boss will look around for you, someone will state that you have stepped out, and he will move onto the next issue at hand. By the time you are back, he will be so immersed in beating up the operations head on the call centre failures that you will be forgotten.

Make sure that you don't return too early—nothing worse than hearing, 'Good. You're back at just the right time. What's with the high attrition last month?'

Chew well and swallow

Always have your mouth full of meeting snacks and if you get asked a question, hold out your hand and request for a moment—the thirty recommended chews before each swallow should buy you time to think up an answer. If you are eating Oreos, you get even more time because it's acceptable to first lick off the cream, then eat the cookie, and then start answering.

Pre-empt and go offline

Anticipate difficult questions and pre-empt them by declaring that you don't have the answers, even before they are asked. As soon as you see a prospective nemesis readying to launch his missile, weave a pre-emptive sentence into your script: 'Now, I don't know what XYZ exactly is, but I do know that...' Once you have declared this, someone would have to be idiotic to go ahead and ask the question anyway, and in all likelihood, they will let it pass.

If you do get asked a difficult question and pre-emption hasn't worked, try post-emption with a confident 'I'll get back to you.' No one ever gets back to anyone—I'm still waiting for some colleagues from my first job twenty years ago to get back to me.

Finally, if you are desperately losing a verbal duel with a colleague, extricate yourself with, 'Let's take it offline.' No one knows where offline is and nothing ever gets back online but it's the corporate equivalent of waving a white flag. 'I'm looking like an idiot here in front of our boss. Have mercy. I will make it up to you.' Gracious warriors sheath their swords when they hear this plea.

Shine by echoing

Sometimes, the boss will ask a question to the room and even if you are clueless, you can shine by following a strategy I call 'Echoing'. Avoid eye contact and stare into space pretending to think as he looks around expectantly. As soon as someone begins answering, start repeating the answer after him. The timing is critical—you must begin to echo the answer before the other person completes it.

Boss: Does anyone know which state had the highest sales last quarter?

Avoid any eye contact as everyone in the room thinks and the honcho looks around awaiting a response.

Intelligent Colleague: Sir, it is West Be...

As soon as you hear West Be..., you figure out the answer and start repeating 'West Bengal'. By the time the colleague has said the 'gal' of 'Bengal', you are starting the 'Ben' and you finish not more than a few seconds later. From the boss's perspective, you both knew the answer but the other muppet happened to blurt it out faster.

The risk is that West Bengal may not be correct but you have hedged your bet. There are two of you who believe that it had the most sales last quarter and chances are that a couple of other colleagues would have started echoing too. So even if it happens to be wrong, who cares?

Altercast and turnaround

Have an annoying colleague who asks too many questions? Force them into a role where he or she will feel compelled to act accordingly. 'How can an intelligent and time conscious executive like you raise such trivial questions?' The dumbarassed chump will think twice before interrupting the meeting the next time to ask you anything.

If some junior stumps you with his question, turn it around by asking, 'What do you think?' Your seniority entitles you to first get his view and basis his response, you may get some insights into what the answer should be. If you are still clueless, murmur 'Hmm' and move onto the next topic.

Asking Questions

And there will be times when you need to look wise and differentiate yourself through your questions, especially when interacting with senior management. Let's explore how to do this in the context of town hall meetings.

The Town Hall meeting

This is standard operating procedure to keep early careers and mid-management involved. All employees are called into the cafeteria or conference hall and the CEO and senior executives blabber on stage on topics they deem important to share with the organization at large. The good news is that town halls rarely go wrong—it's relatively easy to hide amongst a sea of people and look interested. But equally, it is an excellent opportunity to stand out and you can do so by flooring the leadership in the mandatory question and answer session at the end.

Audience questions are either planted or extempore. Planted questions are framed in advance by HR or Internal Communications, blessed by the executives who'll be answering them and given to select articulate employees in the audience. Ensure that you are one of the plantees. Practise the tone, pitch and pronunciations beforehand so that you don't slur or goof up when you go on air. When you ask the question, shuck and jive as if it's an original query. Everyone knows that it is a charade but the leadership will reciprocate by acting as if they're thinking hard before they answer.

Extempore ones are more challenging. Firstly, the bar is raised as you are dealing with confident leaders who don't need queries planted. Secondly, you have to come up with something intelligent on your own. Most people make the cockamamie mistake of asking questions that will stump the leader in public. Why would one ever want to do that? Instead ask questions that he can smoothly answer and look presidential, authoritative and brilliant. Stay away from touchy topics like appraisals, raises, promotions, restroom cleanliness or canteen food and stick to themes around CVC—Customer, Vision, and Competition.

Customer: Questions around the customer make the leader appear kind, considerate and well intentioned. There will be a hush in the room and one can almost hear light jazz playing in the background as he remarks on soft balls such as:
- How can we be more customer-centric?
- How do you see consumer trends and behaviours changing over the next few years?

Vision: Every leader believes that he has an awesome strategic vision, so give him an opportunity to share it. Ask him a suitable question and watch as he clears his throat, adjusts his tie and launches into his address.
- Could you share your three-year vision for our company?
- What do you think digital and social media is doing to help our organization?
- In your view, what's the long-term impact of the government's recent economic measures on our industry?

Competition: To raise the tempo of the room a few notches, ask him about competition. Nothing fires up a good old leader more and you might even cause a war cry to break out across the room.

- What do you think we can do better than competition?
- What do you think the competition is working on presently?
- Who do you think will be our biggest competitor ten years down the line?

China: Lastly, if others have beaten you to the above before your waving hand was spotted, pull out the secret weapon in your arsenal—China. You can never go wrong with China. Ask whether your industry has a threat from China and then step back proudly as the gasps of admiration reverberate around you.

These *Ask an Awesome Question* tricks can be used in town halls, job interviews or any other senior interaction. The objective is to ask simple, straightforward, 'ball coming nicely onto the bat' questions that will have them heave a silent sigh of relief. Their appreciation will be reciprocated with a 'That's an excellent question,' before they launch into an answer that no one is registering. But they have registered you.

In Conclusion...

Your aim throughout your career should be to question a lot and answer little. Use your left-brain logic and objectivity to ask questions and your right-brain creativity and imagination to answer them. It's a skill that will develop through sustained practice; don't shy away from it.

10

NAVIGATING BUSINESS REVIEWS

Strategies to ride out the toughest of inquisitions

No matter which function you work with, you will be subjected to regular reviews where your boss will try to catch out your incompetence and you will attempt to disguise it. Let's uncover some strategies to sail through them in the context of the sales function, simply because the quantifiable nature of sales lends itself to a culture of frequent business reviews. The lessons however apply to all departments. Please sit up and sell me your ears.

As a salesperson, your month starts with a target, budget or plan and you are then tracked like a hawk, your inputs and outputs closely monitored and your lack of performance evaluated. This kind of open kimono lifestyle is not particularly exhilarating, especially when your sole objective is to stay under the radar and therefore the key to success is opacity. Keep everything confidential and murky— your location, prospects, strategy and calendar. Everything should be treated with top-level secrecy because ambiguity cannot be probed.

I won't teach you how to become a formidable sales professional; many esteemed authors have written tomes on that stuff. But I will guide you on crawling out of the big hole that you'll find yourself in when you discover that the garbage in these books doesn't work. When you miss your targets yet again and your boss is going to Bruce Lee your backside in the upcoming review, that's where I'll step in—to help you not just survive, but shine.

Managing the Projection Cycle

You can't avoid reviews altogether but can postpone them by over-managing the projection cycle. In sales, like much of life, it's not what you deliver that stays top of mind but what you promise to deliver. Sales organizations run on projections and you will frequently be asked for your deal pipeline and estimates. Even if you have no clue about what you'll achieve, you certainly control what you project.

Delay any bad news until the very end and start the month with nothing other than supreme confidence about meeting targets. In fact, dangle a carrot of potential over-delivery and your boss will leave you unbothered. At mid-month, your projection should be almost as exuberant but just leave things as being 'nicely on track'. Maintain this optimism until the third week when you should mildly surface some early concerns. 'The team is facing some challenges, nothing major.' Step up the rhetoric a few days before month-end and simultaneously lay the foundation for next month—'It looks like we are going to be short but I'm already on top of next month like a gorilla in heat.'

Avoid crossing paths with the boss in the last week of the month. In case he does accost you in the corridor, do a boomerang—rather than talk about your failures, put him on the spot by making him accountable and responsible for your success. 'Boss, I really need your urgent help with some approvals from finance. Can I schedule a meeting with you, the CFO and my team?' He will go on the defensive, murmur an uncertain okay and avoid you for the next few days. No one likes to work. Even your boss.

Navigating the Review

While the above should buy you some time, consistent under-delivery will eventually get you hauled into the conference room. It's not a big deal. Go into the review projecting confidence. Know where the goalposts are and understand that your underperformance is not as severe as it seems. It's customary for each layer of management to buffer the target it rolls out. The CEO receives a target of X from the board but he doubles it to 2X for the national sales head so that even if he gets halfway there, the CEO makes his bonus. The national head doubles it to 4X for his regional heads with the same logic who make it 8X for state heads. By the time it reaches the individual salesperson on the ground, the original target of X has been buffered more than a PornHub video on a dialup connection. You can very well roll your eyes when he questions your under achievement against this utterly hypothetical target.

Don't go in unprepared. Just as your boss expects to receive your presentation before the review, ask him for his questions in advance. Get a sense of what approach will he take to beat you up and explain that you would rather develop plausible excuses beforehand than make up random stuff on the spot.

Irrespective of how bad things are, leave him with some positive key messages. Let's assume that you are the northern region sales head for Cottony Crotch Co and you have missed your underwear sales targets yet again for the month. After deliberating with your team over heated calls and whisky, you have devised the following three messages that you want to convey to your boss:

1. **Palm off Bad Performance:** Most of the customers were on holiday for Diwali so we missed our targets

2. **Sell false hope:** With Christmas around the corner, demand for red underwear should increase significantly and we will over-deliver here on

3. **Demonstrate creativity and bias for corrective action:** I have mandated no solid foods until dinner for the entire sales team. With this, people won't waste time taking dumps during the day and productivity will go up

Once you have the key talking points, use every opportunity to reiterate them. Personal anecdotes keep things interesting.

'My wife and I recently went on a detox and consumed only juices for a week. We were much more efficient since we didn't waste time in the bathroom. That got me thinking about the potential impact this could have on an entire sales force if they only took bathroom breaks for Number 1 and not Number 2. I have therefore mandated no solid foods until dinner; our productivity lift from this will be 10 per cent.'

Statistics provide credibility:

'Our typical salesperson goes for a dump about ten times a week. The average job lasts eight minutes and increases by three minutes if the dumper takes his phone along.'

Always move from the difficult questions that you have been asked to answers that you want to give, by bridging to your key messages. Helpful phrases such as 'But the main challenge...', 'However, it's important to remember...' and 'Keep in mind that...' help achieve this.

> **Boss:** 'Why was North the worst performing region for the fifth quarter in a row?'
>
> **You:** 'Yes, performance has been little below par but the main challenge that we are focusing on now is productivity. To fix this, I have mandated no solid foods until dinner. Our productivity lift will be 10 per cent.'

Give the boss enough mundane information to get him off your back. As Voltaire said, 'The best way to be boring is to leave nothing out.' Inundate him with minute details about everything. You will notice the tell-tale signs of him losing all interest in your lack of achievements. He will go expressionless, start admiring his fingernails and shoes, fiddle with his phone, stifle a yawn and soon won't even bother suppressing it.

Always stagger good news. Rather than sharing that 'the motivated team achieved its revenue target with lower expenses' in one statement, split it into three distinct achievements.

- Our team is as charged up as it has ever been

- We have delivered our revenue targets
- We have shown cost consciousness with expenses lower than budgeted

But give bad news all at once, combining it into one long sentence and speaking as fast as you can. 'Revenue was almost there and expenses slightly higher but the team is in place and we assure you that we will do much better next month. SIR!'

Sometimes if you run out of excuses, try 'no comment' as a response.

> Boss: 'Why was North the worst performing region for the fifth quarter in a row?'
> You: 'No Comment.'
> Boss: 'What do you mean, No comment!'
> You: 'I've already given every possible reason. I have no more comments.'

For abysmal news, use the Hamburger Technique. The terrible news is the patty, which you should sandwich between two pieces of good news buns.

'Boss, rumours are that you are going to get a promotion pretty soon. By the way, we totally blew last month and had huge shortfalls that we don't expect to make up in this lifetime. Oh, and your wife called, she has asked you to pick up some KY Jelly and condoms on the way home tonight.'

Excuses for Not Meeting Targets

While they may vary somewhat by industry, in most cases you can give the four primary reasons for missing targets.

Price: Blame the pricing—'We have a good product but our competitor has something identical at 20 per cent cheaper.' It's difficult to argue with a less expensive option and while your boss will try and give some flimsy counters, he really doesn't have a leg to stand on.

Product: If the price is competitive, blame the product. List all the features it doesn't have and position those as the make or break factors in every customer's purchase decision. 'If we only had this missing feature that our competitor offers, we wouldn't be losing so many sales at the last leg.' It usually takes a long time to change product specifications and if you consistently pound the message that your product sucks, you get a lot of runway.

Promotion: You can always blame marketing. 'We are simply not advertising enough. Our competitors are all over television, press, internet but our marketing team is doing nothing. Our brand awareness is negligible.' You have likely touched a raw nerve and are validating what your boss has always suspected—that marketing faffs around all day. Don't be surprised if he clenches his fists as you rant about your struggles on the field.

Processes: Finally, you have the processes to fault. Most people hate marketing but all people hate operations. Blame the shoddy, archaic and unfriendly processes and you will encounter instant commiseration. Operations is a black box that even your boss can't open.

Muddle the Sales Formula

Let's assume you have a ten member sales team, the average sales person sells twenty briefs a month (productivity) and each brief is priced at Rs 300 on average (average ticket size). The total sales volume therefore is

Sales = Average Ticket Size X People Selling X Productivity
= Rs 300   X 10   X 20
= Rs 60,000

Total sales, therefore, is a function of average ticket size (how much each sale is worth), the number of people selling (more sales people, more sales) and productivity (the more a person sells, the higher the sales volume).

If you have a quantitative boss deep diving into your abysmal performance, muddle him on these levers of the sales formula. If he enquires about your dismal Average Ticket Size, talk about people. 'We are facing a hiring challenge and need more underwear salespeople. HR is doing nothing.'

If he starts questioning you on people, talk about productivity. 'Many people were on sick leave so productivity dipped. However, our viral video on thongs has generated numerous leads and we should see productivity lift.'

And if he questions productivity, talk about the challenges with Average Ticket Size. 'Customers are preferring to go commando and are spending less on underwear. The average ticket size has therefore fallen significantly.'

Do this muddle and switch effectively and you will eventually beat him into weary submission and he will drop the detailed questioning. And that will be the end of the review.

In Conclusion...

Whether it is sales or any other function, reviews will be an integral part of corporate life. Like with most other things, preparation and confidence are crucial. Remember that only you know the true extent of your incompetence and your boss will merely be drawing cues from your answers, so misguide him appropriately. Always stand by your misstatements. Understand the levers of your business so that you can play around with them. Never give straight answers to anything— the most successful employees never answer any question directly even though they can talk for hours, keeping you fully engaged. Remember that the overarching objective in all reviews is to swing things such that you answer not what you are asked, but what you want to answer.

PERCEPTIONS AND DECEPTIONS

11

MANAGING INTERNAL PERCEPTIONS
Creating realistic false personas

Most people make the mistake of lavishing attention only on their immediate boss but effective politicking demands that you manage perceptions all around—your colleagues, subordinates, seniors and so on. Organizations are lumbering elephants with long memories and you never know when, where and with whom your paths will cross. So it's better to keep your bridges mostly un-burnt with all.

The easiest way to look good is to surround yourself with mediocrity. Seek organizations and teams that are infested with average talent and by default, you'll appear a star. A diamond shines in the rough, a lotus blooms in the muck, and even a middle-of-the-road dolt is an achiever when others are waddling on the footpath. But if you are in an environment where colleagues are even somewhat competent, you will have to put in extra effort to stand out.

You will get many opportunities to do that but you just need to know where to strike and what pitfalls to avoid.

Dress Management

Close your eyes and think of the corporate professional whom you most admire. Now visualize him or her squatting, unkempt, in a sleeveless vest and striped pyjamas—does he or she still look as awe-inspiring? Various research has validated that your dress dramatically influences how people perceive you, so go get those mothballs of the suits dusted.

Early careers and mid-managers should strike the right balance between shabby and well groomed. Dress like a pauper and no one will take you seriously but dress too well and resentful colleagues will believe that you are overpaid, the boss will assume that you have family wealth and Compliance will suspect that you're moonlighting on the side. Take the middle path to dressing with standard shirts and trousers and off-the-rack suits. If you wear anything fancy, spread the word that it was purchased at a sale, practically for free. Avoid loud colours and bold prints; nothing you wear should be memorable, either for how good or bad it was. But do compliment co-workers if they are wearing ridiculous outfits and let them know that you could never match their unique style.

At work, males should remove their jackets and roll up shirt sleeves half way between the wrist and elbow, not all the way up as that's very management trainee-like. Loosen the tie to round off the 'I'm extremely hands-on, neck deep in work but loving it' look. For females, I'm not sure what the equivalent is. Tie your hair up in a tight bun with a few loose strands dangling across your forehead—that always looks so 'I'm so-in-charge busy'.

Wear thick rimmed spectacles and even if you have rabbit perfect vision, fit plain lenses—no one other than your optician needs to know. According to a survey by the London Vision Clinic, people look three to five years older on average if they wear glasses. Carry a rolled-up newspaper under your armpit, perch your glasses on your nose and peer around. Occasionally remove your spectacles and elegantly chew on the temple of the frame. You scream intelligence.

 As a senior leader, remember that your position is aspirational and people expect you to live in the penthouse and drive the Jag. Don't dash their aspirations. Dress for success, projecting an air of self-confidence with your sharp suits, smart shoes and designer accessories. 'But I can't afford haute couture,' the middle-class mindset in you will scream. Let me teach you how to look like a million bucks, every day for the rest of your life, for lesser than what you spend on your daily biscoot. The *Job Be Damned DICK* (Daily Incremental Cost of being a King) concept will forever change the way you look at consumption.

DICK calculates the incremental cost, per use, of buying something awesome rather than shoddy and if reasonable, advises purchasing awesomeness. To illustrate, let's assume that a run of the mill tie costs Rs 1,000 while a designer tie costs Rs 6,000. The additional cost therefore is Rs 5,000 (6,000 – 1,000). Let's assume that you will wear this tie once a week for four years which is about ~200 usages (52 X 4). The incremental cost of wearing a designer tie each time is therefore only ~Rs 25 (Rs 5,000 / 200 occasions). Now isn't Rs 25 worth the satisfaction of having co-workers stop in their tracks, reach over and flip your stunning tie around to examine the label?

You can DICK your entire wardrobe and calculate the daily incremental cost of replacing all your riff-raff with high quality luxury brands. You will see that for less than Rs 300 a day, you can while away time with a permanently decadent aura of self-confidence around you. What are you waiting for?

Establishing Power

Now that you are looking spiffy, enhance your perception by displaying power with your behaviour and body language.

The only accessory that you should need in your job is your scheming brain; anything more and you are still a flunk. Don't carry a laptop and never take notes in meetings—that's for losers. Quietly sit back, mentally absorbing the main points, as you swivel your chair in 45-degree arcs. Press the pen so hard that the nib breaks when you write; all will be in awe. Walk confidently—imagine a massive explosion behind you, cars flying, a pistol in each hand as you stride in slow motion; that should be your gait as you stride around the office. Golf is synonymous with power and while your lame co-workers are hitting pretend cricketing cover drives, swing an imaginary golf club and watch, hand capping forehead, as the imaginary golf ball flies an imaginary three hundred yards.

Lions, kings of the animal kingdom, use urine to mark out their territories in a process called scent marking. The strong smell of their piss lingers on, essentially conveying their territorial information to other felids who may come by. While I'm not suggesting that you urinate in their cabins, you should clearly establish your territory with co-workers. Meetings should only be held in your workspace or as a compromise, in conference rooms. But never walk into anyone else's cabin, unless it is, and I am not advocating this, to piss.

Have a signature signal to indicate displeasure to colleagues. One can't slam doors in open layout offices and a gentle right to left swipe doesn't have the same impact as banging down a phone. Work out some other action that establishes that you are stewing in anger. Jabbing a paper cutter on their hands or spitting on their shoes are options. People should be so conditioned that as soon as they hear you clear your throat, they know that they are in deep trouble.

Finally, any association with change management puts you onto a fast track career path. Not because change management is a critical corporate activity but it just sounds highly important. 'Wow, he is a change manager—if he can manage change, he can manage anything.' If anyone asks what you exactly do, let them know that you are analyzing what needs to be changed and then you will change it. Make eye contact, look cold and evil, make a mock pistol with your hand and cock it up and down a few times. The pesky buzzard will back off.

Perception Management

While your overall appearance and demeanour will go a long way in determining what people think of you, other situations can either shred your perception or enhance it. Your colleagues will be expending their valuable energy in mundane tasks such as attending meetings, meeting targets, targeting promotions and so on. Let them waddle along the feckless corporate journey while you utilize your time to go the extra mile, in situations such as the following.

Smoking is not injurious to career

Smokers know that puffing every cigarette at work typically involves 25 steps.

1. Put computer to sleep
2. Walk from your desk to your smoking buddy's cubicle
3. Wait for him to wrap up whatever he is doing
4. Walk to coffee machine
5. Make two coffees
6. Walk from coffee machine to elevator
7. Take elevator to ground floor
8. Walk to parking lot
9. Hand over coffee cup to him as you light your cigarette
10. Hold his coffee cup as he lights his cigarette
11. Puff cigarette
12. Sip coffee
13. Gossip
    -- Repeat steps 11 to 13 until cigarette is over --
14. Stub cigarette
15. Discard coffee cups
16. Ask around for a mint. No one has one.
17. Go to paan shop and buy a mint
18. Walk to elevator
19. Take elevator up
20. Go to restroom

21. Wash hands
22. Gargle
23. Pop in mint
24. Drop smoking buddy back to his desk and walk back to your cubicle
25. Awaken computer

It seems like a lot of effort for the momentary pleasure of puffing on a cancer stick and doing this many times a day could even label you as a shirker. But what most people miss is that this entire routine involves a smoking buddy and imagine if that happens to be your boss. It's rare to get this kind of quality time with him—shimmying to the coffee machine, intimately holding each other's cigarettes, gossiping, giggling and even gargling together—it's an incredible perception-boosting opportunity. And even if your boss doesn't smoke, smoking in itself is excellent for your career. You can expect to kick the bucket many years before non-smokers, thereby getting out of this crappy rat race early. It's a win-win situation.

Birthday Celebrations

Childish as they are, birthday celebrations are an integral part of corporate life. The team faithfully gathers in the canteen, sings as the birthday person blows out candles, smiles politely as the boss says a few words and then everyone has a slice of cake and leaves. It is a seemingly simple activity that doesn't deserve a second thought but nothing could be further away from the truth. All birthday celebrations involve two critical activities that you should watch out for.

1. **Cutting the cake:** Once the birthday person has blown the candles and *Happy birthday* has been sung out of tune, it's decision time. Who will cut the cake into pieces so that everyone can dig in? Cake cutting is a menial, thankless task and it shouldn't matter who does it, as long as it's not you. What is one even doing exactly—equitably divvying up a geometrical cake into the required number of slices? Indulging in this act screams that you are willing to take on useless responsibilities and as you cut so shall you reap. Subconsciously, everyone will consider you the team flunky who is to be loaded with the tasks that no one wants to do—crappy projects, printing and binding jobs, photo copying, etc. Leave the cake cutting to someone else and if no one makes a move, let it rot on that canteen table.

2. **Smearing the cake:** It is a waste of dessert but people smear a perfectly good slice of cake on the birthday person. Usually everyone looks to the boss to do the smearing; it's least controversial and you should let him do the honours. But sometimes, seniors aren't inclined to indulge in such juvenile activities. It's then that you must grab the opportunity and a slice, and jump in to do the smearing. It's instant recognition for you as the go-to guy who can get his hands dirty—literally and metaphorically.

   However, if it's your boss's birthday, stay in the background as everyone looks around sheepishly for someone to coat his face with icing. And when no one steps forward, wait for the team lackey, as identified above, to start cutting the cake into equal slices.

The concept of not being the team loser applies not just to cake cutting but any other 'office housework' activity. Do you have team breakfasts on Fridays and are you the one lugging in kachoris for the entire unit? Do you have best decorated department competitions at Diwali and are you painstakingly coordinating lights and decorations for the whole team? Are you the dependable person everyone turns to whenever some group activity needs to be organized? Why don't you just designate yourself Chief Loser Officer on your business card?

Office Farewells

Ever so often, you will have colleagues who will find a job elsewhere, thereby proving that 'there is always a bigger sucker' organization. It is an incredible blow to the ego, especially since you have been trying to get out for far longer than they have but make the best of it. Immediately position yourself as the next in line go-to guy and one of the best places to do this is at their farewell.

The leadership sometimes hosts farewell parties for important leavers. It's the usual dog and pony show— cocktails, snacks and people milling around conversing with the leaver and the seniors. At some point in the evening, someone takes a spoon and clinks their whisky glass, 'Attention, Attention, it's time for a few words' and people gather around to share their thoughts about the fortunate leaver. It is imperative that you also give a farewell speech.

An archetypal farewell speech has the speaker reminiscing about the time spent with the leaver and expounding on her virtues. The issue is that it's completely irrelevant—no one cares about your emotions for an employee who is anyway leaving. Nor does anyone care how good at her work she was, especially since another organization is going to benefit from it hereon. Your target audience for the speech is the senior leadership present as rarely will you get such an opportunity to have them listen, undistracted, to you. So in the garb of praising the leaver, position yourself awesomely.

Talk about your learnings from the leaver thereby reiterating the key skills that you have. 'Everything I know about time management, which I do exceedingly well now, is thanks to Rupa and the discipline she inculcated in me.'

Highlight some of the leaver's successful projects and squeeze in some credit for yourself. 'As an integral part of the Project Tulip team, which reduced our operating costs by 30 per cent, I was indeed privileged to work with Rupa closely.'

Limit the organizational impact of the leaver's departure to drab and meaningless items, thereby giving the leadership comfort that it's no great loss. 'What we will miss most about Rupa is her attention to details—the coffee machines on our floor never ran out of pods thanks to her.'

Finally, project yourself as the go-to company man and unofficial guardian of her legacy. 'Rupa don't worry—I promise you that I will ensure that your role and the department go to greater heights even with you not there.'

Many of your shy colleagues will avoid making a farewell speech, choosing to give a limp handshake to Rupa on the sidelines instead. You now know better, so step up and grab that microphone.

Idea Generation Schemes

Sometimes you will receive an HR mailer, filled with clipart of light bulbs, about an employee initiative called *Nayee Disha*, *Hamari Soch*, *Think outside the box*, etc. It's an idea generation scheme where employees are asked to submit ideas around themes like removing bureaucracy, reducing expenses, growing revenues or improving processes. The five best submissions will supposedly be implemented and winners will get certificates and a cool pair of shades from the CEO.

Should you even bother participating? The reality is that no one cares two hoots about your ideas and it's also very unlikely that you will suggest anything that hasn't been already rejected in the past. This is simply a way to keep HR occupied and they will measure success on the basis of the quantity, not quality, of ideas generated. However, the irrelevance of this exercise should not dissuade you and grab the opportunity to differentiate yourself.

Here's my idea. Submit 100 plus ideas—literally. This itself will be a talking point for the HR head in the next leadership meeting—'A young man from Finance has sent in 130 ideas,' and he will thump his chest as if he was the one orchestrating your brainwaves. Copy your department head on your submissions. Seniors love to show a connection with youth and he will proudly bandy your emails, noting that he has the pulse of the organization throbbing in his varicose veined wrists.

Keep your brainwaves simple—switch off lights at night, sell more stuff to increase revenues, spend less to save expenses and such. Write in kindergarten-level English because some junior HR twits, without knowledge of business or jargon, will have been given the responsibility of reading all submissions. The ideas don't even have to be original or exceptionally bright—the best ideas are the ones that have already been implemented. Has your department recently changed any process? Recycle it as a new concept. Some cost-cutting efforts already been made? There you go—Innovations 2,3 and 4 right there. So just submit some initiatives that are already ongoing—HR will announce them as winners, the leadership will pretend to execute them, and you can update your CV with a *Winner of Nayee Disha employee initiative* bullet.

Summer Internships

If your organization has internship programmes wherein students come in over the summer to undertake projects, take one under your wing. Not only do you get the cheapest form of white-collar labour to slave for you but also earn brownie points with HR for whom this programme is one of the year's most challenging tasks. Now you may be concerned about how to keep your ward gainfully occupied for an entire summer and here's a standard, eight-week *Job Be Damned* internship schedule that you can follow.

Week 1 **Settling in:** Welcome your intern with a polite, 'Who the heck are you?', introduce him to your team and then leave

him alone for the rest of the week. He needs to coordinate luxuries such as a desk, computer, ID card with HR and Admin and this takes time.

Week 2 **Assisted Orientation:** When he timidly knocks, wave him in and provide him with all the books, presentations and articles that are lying around. Ask him to come up the curve on the industry and clean out your desk in the bargain.

Week 3 **Unassisted Orientation:** Ask him to expand his research through external sources and surfing the internet. IT has likely denied him internet access for security reasons, but he surely has a personal dongle.

Week 4 **Project Introduction:** He must be anxiously chomping at the bit by now and halfway into the summer, he should probably get started on a project. If you don't have any better ideas, *Competitive Analysis* is a good standard internship topic. Jot down a list of competitors and variables that he should research. Hint at the prospect of him receiving a pre-placement interview offer if he also does a SWOT analysis and makes that the dog-cow-whatever matrix.

Week 5 **Midterm review:** Stress him by asking him to present the work done so far which obviously is nothing. Express irritation at his slow speed and ask him to double up efforts; nothing like some real-world pressure to give him an authentic experience of corporate life. If you have budgets, take him out for a team lunch; if not, he can continue to eat alone in the canteen as he has been doing for weeks.

Week 6 **Field Work:** Check if he has visited customers, distributors, branches, factories, etc., which he obviously hasn't since no one asked him to. Watch him gasp and gulp with wide eyes— it is a lot of fun.

Week 7 **Presentation preparation:** He should work on his end-of-project report, which will largely be a collation of neatly formatted blank slides given the utterly unstructured approach that you have adopted. But don't be concerned—he is a future *You* and will improvise.

Week 8 **Assessment:** Have him present his project to you and anyone else willing to sit through an hour of nothingness. Nod all the while, thank him for his effort and assure him that you will implement his recommendations. You won't hear from him again and vice versa.

Corporate Social Responsibility (CSR)

The objective of corporate social responsibility is to serve the community and there are some wonderful examples. Philip Morris, the world's largest cigarette manufacturer, claims to be a top 10 per cent leader for climate change and reduction of harmful gases in the environment. Monsanto, widely recognized for its excellent work in genetically modifying foods and seeds, allegedly creating ghastly environmental disasters and allegedly leading thousands of farmers to suicide, has a lovely 70+ page sustainability report outlining its social work for people and the planet. These are some positive examples but in most other cases, CSR is a farce purported to show an imaginary softer side of organizations in websites and annual reports.

Now if your company is hell bent upon showing its inner warmth to the world, jump onto the bandwagon and attend every volunteering activity that is organized. These are not time consuming and invariably revolve around the typical feel-good stuff—teach kids, talk to elderly people, paint classrooms and so on. Sometimes you may even have to build something like a library or hospital room but all comforts will be taken care of as you partake in manual labour. Air-conditioned buses to transport you, food to keep you nourished, drinks to keep you hydrated, caps to keep you cool and T-shirts to make everyone look coordinated. Members of the leadership will be there with their families to evidence that their entire clan is oh-so-caring. Look suitably impressed.

While you are labouring, photographs will be taken for the website and other collaterals. Sidle into as many as possible; you want to be noticed as someone deeply entrenched in CSR. These are serious corporate mugshots meant to evoke sympathy and you need to display only one emotion in every snap—believable compassion. Carry a crying baby in your arms, hold the hand of an elderly man lying on a hospital bed, or artistically paint a crumbling wall—whatever it is, look into the camera with liquid, moist eyes, chin jutting out and fists clenched, as you do it. The PR team will sift through thousands of photographs to narrow down on the few that will make the final cut and the more tired yet believably compassionate you look, the higher the chances of your career rocketing. If you are really lucky, you may even be adopted by a visiting global or regional office executive (more on them in the chapter on Jonathan Visiting Seagull) and taken back to his home country to display similar compassion.

In Conclusion...

As the French novelist Gustave Flaubert wrote, 'There is no truth, only perception.' Perception is the way in which something is regarded, understood or interpreted and it doesn't matter who you are, as long as people think what you want them to think that you are. Every nuance of the way in which you conduct yourself shapes what people think of you. So, focus on managing your perception—it is the most important thing you will ever manage in your career.

FEEL GOOD ANECDOTES

The spy who fooled me

A prime example of managing perceptions comes from the world of espionage where a chicken farmer managed to fool the Nazi regime into believing that he was one of their best secret agents ever.

Juan Pujol Garcia was a poultry farmer turned hotel attendant in Madrid during World War II. There was nothing more that he wanted than to spy for the Allies against the Nazis. He approached the Brits multiple times pleading for a job but finding absolutely no 007 qualities in him, the balding Spaniard was rejected each time. Rather than going back to working room service, he decided to try his luck with the Germans and set up a clandestine meeting with one of their foremost spy runners and pitched his espionage services. Name-dropping more fervently than an aunty at a South Extension kitty party, he convinced the Germans to hire him and was asked to relocate to Britain and spy for them.

Probably not a fan of the balmy UK weather or their unhealthy diet of fish and chips, Pujol instead relocated to Lisbon, Portugal. He proceeded to buy all the UK guidebooks and maps he could lay his eyes on and subscribed to all available British newspapers and magazines. Using this research material, he started drafting highly detailed but completely imaginary reports that he sent to his German handlers, all the while pretending to be travelling around Britain. He even 'recruited' a team of twenty-seven fictitious associates to help him and submitted travel expense reimbursement claims for the entire team using restaurant menus and train timetables from newspapers. In all, he claimed a total of over $350,000 in expenses—millions of dollars in today's money—for their 'work'.

The detail exhibited in his reports allayed any doubts the Nazis might have had. His information, based purely on his vivid imagination, was invariably wrong and he cast the blame on his team. But when he happened to be luckily right, he took the credit and further established his reputation. A guess that a convoy of Allied ships was leaving Liverpool for Malta turned out to be accurate, giving jitters to British intelligence who had intercepted the message and launched a manhunt to find the spy who wasn't there.

He was considered by the Nazis as one of their best spies ever and even referred to as the equivalent of a 45,000-man army in an internal German memo. He again reached out to the Brits for a job, and suitably impressed with his knowledge of England, especially since he had never stepped foot in there, they hired him. Now with British help, he proceeded to feed incredible amounts of false data to the Nazis. His most valuable contribution was misleading the Germans that the Allies were mounting an impending invasion of Calais, diverting Hitler's attention from Normandy 300 miles away where the game-changing attack was to take place. Between January to June 1944 when the invasion actually took place, he sent over 500 messages feeding false information that kept the German army distracted. This of course changed the course of the war and saved thousands of lives.

The Germans never realized that they had been fooled and awarded him the Iron Cross for his service to the German war effort, an honour that was authorized by Hitler himself. A few months later, the Brits honoured him with an MBE from King George VI and Pujol was conceivably the only person in World War II to have received decorations from both sides.

Now if that's not perfect perception management, I'm not sure what is.

12

MIDDLE MANAGEMENT SPECIAL: CROAKING EXTERNALLY

From a frog in the well to a toad on the road

 Middle management frogs can have a perfectly average career within the internal well of office politics. But for toads that want to get ahead, nothing suggests senior leadership material more than a display of external focus and the ability to croak beyond your cubicle.

Travel

One of the optimal ways to demonstrate a keen awareness of the outside world is to travel—stay away from the office as much as possible. Visit branches, clients or coffee shops— keep people guessing on where you are and what you are doing. 'Business meetings' is a good catch-all phrase to allay any suspicions. Your bosses will love your dedication, your subordinates will admire your frequent flyer statements and your spouse will appreciate the space.

The downside of corporate travel is that organizations have implemented adequate policies to humiliate you. Pack camping gear when you travel given the measly hotel expense limits that you are allowed. Laundry policies will require you to turn over your underwear inside out a few times before you can officially give it for a wash. Draconian flight policies have you doing the walk of shame to economy class while peers from other organizations sit smugly in business. And when it comes to the entire expense submission process, you will have a better shot at writing novels with your calculator than extracting reimbursements from finance.

Finance professionals undergo specialized training in rejecting employee expense claims. The only opening you have at getting expenses reimbursed is during the last few weeks of the year. The entire finance team is busy with year-end book closing activities and has no time to tally your expenses on cabs and rice plates. So hoard your bills and submit them at one go at year-end, with a tear-jerking apology note and an exception approval from your supervisor. You will get a yelling but at least some money back.

Competitive Analysis

Slip in some facts, data and observations about competitors in any meeting to take your perception up multiple notches.

> Last week our competitor launched their latest product and I tested it. My view is...
>
> I was having lunch with my counterpart in so-and-so competitor and he said...

I investigated that constant sound we hear from the building opposite and it's our competitors laughing at us.

Senior executives are completely detached from ground realities, so give them a few nuggets of market information. Fib if needed, they will never verify it.

Now you can take the old-fashioned route to gathering competitive information—by pounding the streets, reading industry journals, networking with peers or mystery shopping. You could also put some summer interns on the job or have the occasional beer with the salespeople, who hopefully have some idea what competition is doing. But all this requires an inordinate amount of time and hard work, which is avoidable.

The easiest way to get dirt on your competition is from the people who know it the best—the competition. Create an imaginary job opening, reach out to a candidate from competition, schedule an interview, ask him a leading question and then sit back as the puppet spouts example after example about what he is doing at work. You get all the inside scoop and a great sound bite for your next chat with the boss, 'I was interviewing someone from such-and-such competitor last week...'

Conferences and Networking

An industry conference is another excellent opportunity to demonstrate your external focus. It is essentially a paid day off where you get food, drinks and goodie bags to check out hot people from other companies. If you are nominated to attend any of them, grab the opportunity with both legs and scoot.

You will hear senior executives from various companies blather on and your boss might expect a note on the key takeaways from the conference once you are back. That doesn't mean that you need to pay attention all day. The conference schedule will have a summary of what each session is about. Simply cut and paste those as your observations. During presentations, you can daydream until the speaker reaches the final 'Conclusions' slide at which point you should make some token notes. Panel discussions, where a bunch of people aimlessly banter with a narcissistic moderator, are more challenging. But find a seat next to an eager beaver and copy from him as he furiously takes notes.

Conferences usually provide a couple of breaks to mingle with similar uninterested people. This is called networking— the art of judging how useful a person can be to you in the future and deciding whether to exchange cards or slink away. Networking requires a keen ability to make meaningless conversation that seems meaningful. Do some preliminary preparation around four key subjects.

The Stock markets: Have a view on where the markets are heading—'They will be range bound with some volatility.' Pick any one industry that you like—consumer goods, pharmaceuticals, or pickles, and claim that you are 'bullish' on it. Rain always features in any discussion on the economy so have the weather report handy.

Cricket: Know at least seven of the current ten-member national squad and memorize some statistics from their recent matches. Know that the above sentence was incorrect and a cricket team has eleven members. With a 50 per cent probability of getting it right, guess the outcome of their next match. Whenever there's a pause in the conversation, mumble, 'But there will never be another Sachin.'

Politics: Know the main cast of characters including the prime minister, president and finance minister. Have a view on the Gandhis and mutter intermittently, 'Very interesting family. And that Robert I tell you...'

Films: Have at least one personal story about a movie star. Anything that sounds interesting—let's say, you sat next to Raveena Tandon on a flight and wrote a rocking book about air travel where that anecdote featured prominently.

The most difficult part about networking is opening the conversation. How do you introduce yourself to a completely random stranger without sounding idiotic or trying too hard? A fail proof strategy is to walk up to someone and say, 'I don't know anyone here. *Mujhse fraaandship karoge*?' ('Will you make friendship with me?') Most people will be floored by your childlike innocence and sincerity, so please test this without feeling shy.

Training Programmes

Even better than attending conferences is speaking at them and fooling people into believing that you are an expert in some field. If you are invited to speak about anything to an external audience, it makes your lack of knowledge kosher, which is a very good outcome.

Many people get nervous at the thought of delivering training sessions but the trick is to get the audience nicely warmed up. You have scores of strangers in a room who will spend the next few days together and it's important that they get acquainted—do that well and the rest of the session will be a cinch. But that's where most trainers fail. They do the usual mundane ice-breaking activities—hold hands and do jumping jacks, get into groups on the basis of your birth months without talking to one another, etc. It's no wonder that the entire session turns out to be a damp squib. Instead, you should think out of the box and come up with highly effective icebreakers such as the following to get the ball rolling.

Step 1 **Split into groups:** Ask the participants to split themselves on the basis of their favourite sexual position—the missionaries go to one corner, cowboy/cowgirl to another, spooners to a third and so on. To keep it simple, limit them to a few mainstream positions and have one catch-all 'kinkies' for those into BDSM and other like stuff. To prevent confusion, describe each position and you can even place helpful visual posters around the room.

Step 2 **Split further into sub groups:** Once everyone has segregated on the basis of their preferred position, have them further split into subgroups according to their sexual orientation. For example, the missionaries will now divide into three sub-groups: straight, gay or bisexual. As will the spooners, etc.

Step 3 **Split further into pairs:** Now split each subgroup into pairs—pair the straight people into two's—one male, one female, pair the gay males in two's and also the lesbians in two's. Keep the bisexuals as the 'jacks'—they give you a lot more flexibility with their permutation-combination opportunities. For example, a female bisexual could be paired with a straight man or a female lesbian. It makes things easier.

At this point, you should have the entire room segregated into pairs of two people who can conceivably have sex with each other, that too in a position that is preferred by both of them. If there happen to be any singles left without a partner, joyfully exclaim 'Threesome!' and nudge them towards any of the couples. There should be a huge hush of nervousness and anticipation in the room and you could probably hear a pin drop.

Step 4 **Share insights:** Ask the people to turn to their partners, pull out something from their purse or wallet, and explain why it is important to them. After a long pause, confused animated chatter will start. Once time is up, ring a bell and go around the room randomly picking people and asking them to share what they learnt about their partner. You don't have to cover everyone—just a few people. Then ask everyone to disperse and start your main session.

I am not sure how well you will deliver your programme but I can assure you that the audience will be talking about this ice-breaking activity for years.

In Conclusion...

Google displays five times the results when one searches for the importance of focusing internally than it does for focusing externally. I don't need to spell out for you what the majority of your herd-mentality colleagues are doing. You are just one croaker in a large middle management army of frogs, all competing for a few senior leadership positions.

And while everyone is busy battling the chumps within the organization, take some time to meet some fools outside. Your ability to demonstrate external focus may just be the determining factor for whether you will ever be eligible to read the next chapter or not.

13

SENIOR LEADER SPECIAL: EMPLOYEE MANIPULATION

Manipulating with appreciation and meaningless rewards

 Anyone who is not a senior executive is requested to log off this chapter. We are going to be discussing manipulation strategies and insights into our deviousness will give you an unfair advantage.

Great, now that we only have top management reading, here goes: employees need to be kept motivated and engaged, at least occasionally. It's a waste of time because they are really not important. While most corporations rhapsodically claim that their people are their most important asset, it is all bollocks. The most important asset of Google is its search algorithm—if that were to suddenly vanish, all their so-called most important assets would be sitting around doodling home pages in Mountain View. Likewise, the most important asset of Coke is its secret formula. The most important asset of Apple is its products. As the pointy-haired boss in Scott Adams' *The Dilbert Principle* states, employees are in fact the corporation's ninth most important assets, right after carbon paper.

That said, you still might have a few foot soldiers who need to be kept suitably engaged and it's imperative that you identify them rather than waste your efforts in keeping everyone charged up. You can either use complicated psychological tools and personality tests or simply adopt the *Job Be Damned* Boffins and Bozos grid to pigeonhole all your employees.

Motivating the Boffins

Once you have classified all your staff, focus on motivating the boffins.

1. Pretend to care about their development

Employees want to believe that someone gives a damn about them so act as if you do. Learning motivates early careers so pretend to share your vast experience—gift the latest management book or have them attend some wishy-washy training programme. Middle management professionals crave increased responsibility—ironic given that one's sole objective should be to avoid work. Send them on international jaunts, award home-printed certificates and write them LinkedIn recommendations—anything that looks like a progressive step in their career will keep them motivated. The downside of investing in employees is that it makes them more marketable and they might leave to join competitors. However, effect drug-induced amnesia as part of the exit formalities—the ungrateful wretches should forget everything that they learnt at your expense.

Boffins: Must-have employees with useful skills and attributes

Divers	Enthusiastic and eager to please; they dive straight into a project and get it started
Systematics	Masters at organization, creating flow charts, to-do lists, pros and cons columns and schedules
Coordinators	Enjoy directing things along and putting some order into chaos
Specialists	Experts in one particular subject
Conscientious doers	The engine of every team and the ones who do all the real work
Glib communicators	Great at articulating complicated concepts to the people who matter

Bozos: Useless dead-weights who do more harm than good

Gyaani babas	Spout theoretical wisdom unbacked by execution capabilities
Naysayers	Party pooping, energy-draining pessimists who have all the reasons why your plans won't work
Socialists	Mother hens who don't care about what gets accomplished as long as everyone is happy and participating
Conspiracy theorists	Everything about the organization, team and task is a dark conspiracy
Dumbos	Double-digit IQs who incessantly ask irrelevant questions
Spectators	Step back and watch, occasionally piping in with useless suggestions

2. Conduct Employee Engagement Activities

Interacting with personnel is excellent for your morale. Conduct breakout meetings, hang-outs, online chats and parties. Have the occasional whine-and-dine lunch where you swallow the unpalatable canteen food while chatting with them. Keep the interaction one way—you talk, they listen. Have a Q&A session at the end but make a mental note of anyone who has asked you controversial questions and get your revenge in the next appraisal cycle.

3. Charge them up with motivational phrases

Behave like one of those inspirational coaches that you see in sports movies. Give high fives and pat employees on the ass every time they finish a project. Rip off and wave your shirt if the team wins an award. And whenever someone makes a sale, have the entire office jump on him in wild celebration as if he just scored a World Cup goal.

Morale boosting motivational slogans are always popular, though it can be very demanding to keep coming up with new ones. Here is the *Job Be Damned Motivational Quote Generator*, a variant of the popular childhood game 'Name-Place-Animal-Thing', that will give you an adrenalin-racing phrase whenever you require.

The structure of your motivational quote is as follows. Note that these generally sound better in Hindi though English will work almost just as well.

<Name>, tu toh <Animal> hai <Animal>.
Ja, <Place> mein/ko <Thing>

Make one selection from each column to string together your motivational quote.

Name: The person you want to motivate	Animal: Any ferocious creature	Place: Where you want him to create an impact	Thing: What you want to motivate him to do
Rishi	Tiger/ Baagh	Market	Aag laga de (Set on fire)
Ravi	Lion / Sher	Country	Ghutnon bale crush kar de (Get them on knees and crush them)
Uday	Elephant / Haathi	Department	Maar de (Kill)
Manish	Horse / Ghoda	Team	Aasman tak le ja (Take to the skies)
Deepika	Eagle/ Baaz	Competition	Jung jeet ja (Win the war)

Examples:

Ravi, to toh Tiger hai Tiger. Ja, market mein aag laga de.

Or

Deepika, tu toh Eagle hai Eagle. Ja, department ko aasman tak le ja

4. Dangle promotions

Promotions are nothing but a devious play on the human need for recognition. The bitter truth is that one can spend a lifetime within three designations—early career, middle manager and senior leader. However, waiting a decade for each jump isn't very appealing so organizations create various meaningless titles to promote employees at quicker intervals.

Reality	Manipulated Designations
Early Careers (can spend 4 to 8 years in this designation)	Management Trainee (1-2 years)
	Assistant Manager (1-2 years)
	Manager (1-2 years)
	Senior Manager (1-2 years)
Middle Management (can spend 10 to 15 years at this level)	Junior Vice President (2-3 years)
	Assistant Vice President (2-3 years)
	Associate Vice President (2-3 years)
	Vice President (2-3 years)
	Senior Vice President (2-3 years)
Senior Leadership (spend the rest of one's career here)	Associate Director (3-5 years)
	Director (3-5 years)
	Senior Director (3-5 years)
	Managing Director (until sacked)

Many organizations don't give you complete authority over your people actions, instead holding a promotion meeting where the senior leadership gets together to discuss who across the company should be elevated. To ensure that your boffins make the cut, include some bozos as well in your list. They are your sacrificial lambs that will get roundly trashed, but having soundly rejected the first few names you put up, the group will be more receptive to the rest and the boffins will squeak through.

Promotions are best received by employees under duress. Don't hand them out liberally so wait till you see signs of employees getting extremely impatient, even approaching you with external job offers that they have, before you give in to them.

5. Implement simple reward schemes

While annual bonuses and regular promotions go a long way to motivate boffins, supplement them with simple reward schemes, such as sticker charts. These work for all level of employees—from early careers to C-suite executives.

Put up charts in public areas such as cafeterias with the names of participating employees on it. Every time someone does something notable such as finishing an assignment on time, not annoying the regulator or not driving the company into bankruptcy, give that employee a gold star. Set a time frame for the minions to try and collect as many gold stars as they can. At the end of each period, allow them to exchange their stars for instant gratification rewards—three gold stars, for example, could earn fifteen minutes of surfing the internet during office, and five, a box of delicious candy.

Pat star earners on the back or ruffle their hair as you climb a stool to stick the stars on the chart on the wall. They will feel quite emotional.

Yo Mama is <u>M</u>aking <u>A</u>bsolutely <u>M</u>emorable <u>A</u>cronyms

Leaders have to be adept at laying down priorities that the organization can embrace. Replace lengthy memos and boring speeches with crisp messaging that can be easily assimilated by your below-intelligent workforce; catchy acronyms are one way to achieve this. As an example, let's assume that you want all employees to be sharply focused on only five items in their daily lives.

1. **Work**
2. **Health**
3. **Talk**
4. **Eat**
5. **Sex**

Taking the first letter of each priority, see if anything memorable is formed. WHTES, THEWS, SHWET... hmm, nothing really. But hey, if we replace Health with an A-word, we might get something interesting. What's a suitable word that begins with an A? ANALYZE! So, sacrifice Health as a priority and replace it with Analyze for the sake of having an awesome acronym. The revised priorities therefore are:

1. **Work**
2. **Analyze**
3. **Talk**
4. **Eat**
5. **Sex**

Then announce your acronym with great pride and fanfare— 'I am pleased to roll out a new mandate for all employees. There are five priorities that I want everyone to focus on daily at work—**S**ex, **W**ork, **E**at, **A**nalyze, **T**alk—doing all of the above with each other and our customers will ensure that everyone stays happy. So Team, let's **SWEAT**!'

The PETTY approach to retention

When a boffin asks for a few minutes in private, it forebodes an impending 'I want to move on' conversation. Employ the PETTY approach to retention—an elaborate process where you create so many doubts in the leaver's mind that he starts questioning every reason he had for resigning. Leave him so shaken, confused and befuddled that taking no action seems to be the best action of all.

Probe

A smart employee keeps details of his next job confidential but try and extract it so that you can dissuade him appropriately. If he's joining a competitor, ruthlessly criticize their culture, lack of strategy and management. If he's switching industries, ridicule the future of wherever he's going. And if he's considering doing something entrepreneurial, laden him with self-doubt on whether he can handle the pressures of his own venture without your comfortable safety net. If you can't figure out his plans, criticize all of the above—something will stick.

Empathize

Listen, with as much fake sympathy as you can muster, to his reasons for wanting to leave. No matter how ridiculous his concerns seem, promise to address them in the 'medium term'. He doesn't like the job—'I was looking to rotate you anyway once you finish this project.' He doesn't like his colleagues—'I plan to sack most of them and it will just be you, me and a bunch of new folk.' Promise to fix every issue that he raises, tut-tutting that he hadn't highlighted this sooner.

Tempt   Allude that great treasures are in store for him in the next appraisal cycle and you have been discussing top-notch ratings, a huge raise and bonus and possibly an out-of-turn promotion for him. Advise him to hold on for a bit to see what the organization has to offer. If he bites, ready yourself to deal with a betrayed and disillusioned employee when it doesn't happen. But you have at least bought yourself some time to prepare for his imminent departure.

Threaten   If he is still vacillating, throw in a healthy dose of pettiness. Threaten that his exit will be made extremely difficult, every minute of his notice period will be served in slave labour, each rupee invested in him will need to be repaid, he will receive terrible references and his full and final settlement delayed endlessly. Life should look so miserable that any employee will think twice before having the gumption to resign.

Yearn   Now that you have him by the short and curlies, cajole and counsel him to rethink. Lay it on thick and reiterate all the arguments you have made against his decision. Let him know how much you love him. Make him yearn for the falsely bright future that you are shining in his hypnotized eyes. If you've done your job well, the only thing he is resigning to is his fate.

Demotivating the Bozos

While the above will work wonders on the morale of your best performers, you need some strategies to deal with the large group of Bozos who are wasting office oxygen.

1. Sob with them

Bozos always complain. They will perpetually be in your cabin, cribbing about some problem or challenge that they are facing. The best strategy is to weep along, agree with everything they say and even add on your grievances to theirs.

> Bozo: 'Sir, the organization doesn't seem to have a strategy.'
> You: 'You're right. That has been concerning me as well.'

> Bozo: 'Sir, I'm not getting cooperation from my colleagues in other departments.'
> You: 'What do I tell you son, you should see the obstacles I face with my peers. That ass of a CFO and jerk of a CTO I have to deal with—I know exactly how frustrating it must be for you.'

> Bozo: 'Sir, I am swamped—I am working 18-hour days and have absolutely no time for anything outside work.'
> You: 'I completely understand—I have been asking my boss for a day off for the past six months but he still hasn't approved. I haven't seen my kids for weeks. But it's okay—you take next Sunday off.' (sniffle into hanky)

Once bozos believe that your life is even more screwed up than theirs, they will stop complaining.

2. Palm them off to other departments

Ideally, you want bozos to resign but sadly, they rarely leave. Firing them can be messy so instead palm them off to another department, making it seem like you are doing a favour to both the organization and them. Let the receiving unit believe that you are sacrificing one of your best employees. Position it to the bozo as an excellent opportunity to gain cross-functional experience. Let your boss know that you're taking one for the team. Be stoic as you have these conversations; play your cards rights and you will have a happy bozo packing.

Playing your Direct Reports

As you manipulate employees, you may find a select group amongst your direct reports trying to outplay you. They never give straight answers, there is never any bad news and everything seems too good to be true. In fact, the more senior you are, the more you discover that everything around you is maya—an illusion, and you only see a filtered version of the truth that your subordinates want you to see.

To counter-manipulate your directs effectively, you need information. Powerful emperors in history had a network of spies to keep them abreast of relevant happenings on the ground. Police forces around the world cultivate khabris (informers) who give them tips on the going-ons of the underworld. Similarly, develop a small trusted network of enthusiastic early careers that will feed you nuggets of information on what is going on under your oblivious nose. Make unexpected moves like visiting branches and customers unannounced. Play with their minds by holding 'Skip level meetings' where you informally meet your 2-downs, without the directs present, and ply them with alcohol to get office gossip. And then use your new-found knowledge to make completely unwarranted judgements about your directs.

Will all of this help you? Possibly not. But is it what insecure leaders do? Absolutely.

The Power of Data

Power comes from information, and information forms from data and one group of employees controls more data than Mark Zuckerberg. No one knows them. They sit in the basement, five to a desk, working morning to night on pivots, macros and trackers. They are nameless, never invited anywhere and no one celebrates anything. They are likely not even full-time employees but off-roll temps who will wither away unknown. But they have access to data—the nucleus of everything corporate; they are the MIS (Management Information Systems) team.

Be the friend, champion and guide to the MIS team. They can choose what data to make available to you or others, how succinctly or convolutedly to present it and how fast or slow they should work. No one bothers about them anyway and even a marginal interest in their miserable lives will get you their allegiance. And if you control them, you control the information and he who controls the information, controls the organization.

In Conclusion...

When it comes to motivation, remember that equity and fairness are key drivers. People need to believe that they are being treated justly, even if they are not. Fairness is relative and in the absence of comparisons, anything can be passed off as impartial. It's only when they start comparing to colleagues that hell breaks loose. One is thrilled with a promotion until he hears of a colleague who got one faster and his world collapses.

Information asymmetry is therefore critical. Control the information and limit exchanges within the team. Privately, heap all the praise you want but do nothing other than reprimanding and reiterating failings in front of others. Communicate promotions and increments behind closed doors and end each discussion with a request to keep it confidential since you 'haven't made such huge exceptions for anyone else in the team'. Drive an 'each person for himself' culture.

Be clear who your important desk jockeys are and don't waste bandwidth on the rest. Life is too short to experiment with that 'we are all one team' crap. The best senior executives motivate deserving employees, demotivate the useless ones and manipulate everyone.

14

MUDDYING WATERS

Diverting attention by keeping things opaque

Fill a beaker with water and observe how transparent and silent it is. Now add a fistful of mud and shake vigorously till the water is churning and brown. Place it on a table and wait; slowly but surely, the muck starts settling at the bottom and the water goes back to clear. This is the scientific process of sedimentation.

An organization aims to be the beaker of tranquil water, throwing up no surprises. Your goal as an employee is the opposite; never let water remain still long enough for people to figure out what you are up to. When things are hunky-dory they tend to attract attention which is not good. You need to keep buying yourself time and whenever things seem to be settling, shake forcefully and muddy the waters. As you traverse the journey from an early career professional to a senior leader, you will have a range of opaqueness generating options at your disposal.

Early Careers

The beauty of this phase, where you have work without accountability, is that the more work you pretend to take on, the less you need to do.

Join a task force: Joining a cross-functional task force, specially formed to solve some organizational pain point, is a wonderful way to take on faux-work. You will have to do nothing other than attend multiple meetings and pretend to take notes. Your boss will be unable to track your whereabouts as you'll always be huddled in some conference room, and any deliverables can be ignored as you're too junior to be accountable. Your day job will invariably suffer which you can blame on the inordinate time these task forces are consuming. Eventually, the project will fail, a middle manager will get pulled up and you get onto the next task force.

Get two bosses: The more the bosses, the foggier your life and any responsibility that comes with an additional boss is fantastic. While counter intuitive, having two bosses is as good as having none because you can keep playing them. Crib about each to the other, pretend that you are caught up in the other's work and always look exhausted. You will cause the occasional political flare-up between them but don't get caught in the crossfire; be non-committal and it will die down automatically. Let chaos reign and let no one figure out what you actually do or are responsible for.

Middle Management

Once you reach middle management, with even a bit of a reputation as a diligent employee, you have a lot more leeway in muddying the waters. Whenever things seem too calm for comfort, do the following:

Threaten to resign: You may not be the brightest spark in the organizational plug but an unexpected resignation will disrupt, at least temporarily, the smooth life of your boss. You are, after all, the vital link between the early careers who do the actual work and the senior leaders who claim the credit. So, if the pressure is building up, hand in your resignation and listen to the whistle of the cooker go off. The trick is to leave matters open ended enough so that your supervisor has some room to retain you. Give him a flimsy reason for wanting to go—'I want to spend more time with my ailing parents'—and then leave the ball in his court.

Seek a job rotation: Every job has the initial honeymoon period when you are learning. The intermediate phase is that of preparation, when you put the levers in place for a successful outcome. The final stage is execution where having learnt what's needed, you are to deliver as per organizational expectations. Muddy the waters at this crucial juncture and just as you are entering the execution phase, grab any opportunity to scoot before people figure that you can't deliver. Continue doing this for the rest of your career—keep changing roles without accomplishing anything.

Relocate: An alternative is to change geographies. Move from south India to east India, Asia to Europe or London to New York. Relocating is cumbersome and invariably means new cultures, languages, teams and customer behaviours. This provides at least a few years of low expectation, muddied waters for you to wallow in.

Develop a thirst for learning: Foster a sudden desire to up-tier your skills and get your uneducated backside to any executive education programme that your company is willing to sponsor. Leave your present role high and dry while you live it up on a campus. It's very satisfying—getting your boss to pay someone else to teach you the skills to do the job that he's paying you to do.

Switch vendors: Most organizations outsource various activities to external vendors—advertising agencies, payroll processing shops and call centres. Such arrangements are long lasting with the relationship having found its rhythm and chugging along like a well-oiled machine, until a devious manager such as you comes along. Changing vendors instantly muddies the waters as the new partner will take significant time to come up the curve. That buys you time and a foolproof excuse—'The new advertising agency is still learning our brand guidelines and will take a few quarters to be effective.' This year's appraisal is in the bag.

Uncover a corporate scandal: Nothing quite captures the imagination of an organization than some juicy gossip. An accounting embellishment, kickbacks in procurement, the CEO sleeping with the HR head's wife—even a hint of corporate ignominy makes everything else irrelevant. If you can unearth or create a sensational scandal every few years, you will perpetually wallow in mucky waters.

Senior Leadership

As a senior leader, you have tremendous scope and flexibility to obscure the organization's present and future. Use your wide-ranging authority and power to announce game changing initiatives that shroud your team in uncertainty.

Announce a certification exercise: Apply for one of those vague ISO and Six Sigma type quality certifications. A bunch of external auditors will come in and review every process against stringent quality standards and every function will go into a tizzy creating trails, paperwork and process manuals where none existed.

Launch a technology transformation project: If it ain't broke, fix it. Pick one of your company's most important processes or systems and if it is manual, announce that you'll automate it and if it's automated, announce that you'll upgrade it. Create a task force, put the COO in charge and watch anarchy set in. Any technology transformation project invariably overruns on budgets and resources. Also, top management doesn't get sacked in the midst of such projects, so if you have picked the right one to mess around with, you've bought yourself another few years of job security.

Announce a long-term strategic planning project: Sometimes, the best strategy is to strategize and if you can show crystal clear clarity for the future, the present will comparatively be muddy. Launch a long-term strategic plan for the business; something quantifiable yet vague. A Mission $1 billion revenue plan—awesome. By when? Not sure. A three- to five-year strategy plan—great. Is it 3 years, 4 years or 5—don't specify. Don't give away too much information, which shouldn't be difficult since you don't have it anyway. People should appreciate that you are attempting to do something without knowing the time-frames. And no one really cares about the outcome because just like you, they are counting on not being around at the end of it.

Reorganize: Nothing jolts people more out of their complacency and comfort zones than changing their boss or roles. Make the sales head the marketing head and vice versa. Carve out some people from both of them, create a new vertical and fold it under operations. Move Compliance from Risk to Legal, and Procurement from Operations to Finance. Take the org chart home, ask your pre-schooler to redraw the lines, translate her artwork into a radical reorganization and send the announcement email.

Do a retrenchment exercise: Create mass hysteria by announcing a retrenchment exercise—share that 5 per cent of the workforce will be laid off and watch the entire 100 per cent come to a nervous standstill. Panic will set in, projects will grind to a halt, people will crowd around water coolers and speculation will abound as to who all are on the dreaded 'list'. No delivery is expected with employee morale this low and the effects will last for years after the actual lay-offs.

Declare your intent to sell the company: The ultimate scheme to form a whirlpool of muddied water is to mention that the Board is 'evaluating strategic options' for the company. Employees are only focused on their professional future and the uncertainty, stress and general sense of disillusionment will keep things churning for a while.

If you manage to take the organization through a due diligence process where potential suitors and their bankers are poring over your books, congratulations! You may also get a fat retention bonus while this process is underway and you have achieved what very few senior leaders manage to do—get rewarded for muddying the waters.

In Conclusion...

In the age of fake news, nothing is ever what it seems. Politicians, bureaucrats, celebrities, and the media—

everyone is engaging in diverting public attention and there is no reason that you, a wily corporate professional, should refrain from doing so. The ability to effectively cause confusion and create chaos will indeed be a hallmark of your career. So please keep leaving lots of deep and muddy footprints as you stomp up the corporate ladder.

FEEL GOOD ANECDOTES

And with that logic, it's Czech-mate

It was the late nineties and societies were waking up to the serious consequences of smoking. Governments were grappling with the damages caused by puffing cancer sticks, and increasing taxes and tightening regulations to dissuade smokers. The Czech government was also on track to implement some of these initiatives, which wasn't going down kindly with Phillip Morris, the corporation that sold 80 per cent of the cigarettes in this Eastern European chimney.

They decided to muddy the waters with some heart-warming research of their own. They commissioned a reputed management-consulting firm and after intense research, published a report that showed that the Czech smokers were benefiting the government to the tune of $147 million. A lot of this income was coming from increased taxes but also included the savings for the government from lower levels of medical expenses and state benefits drawn by smokers because they simply died earlier than non-smokers. Their death was for a good financial cause, the report concluded.

It was a valiant attempt at muddying the waters. But the outrage and protests resulted in nothing other than mud on their face.

DEALING WITH DISTRACTIONS

15

INSIGHTS INTO OFF-SITES
Everything needed to survive parties and events

While you will spend much of your professional life within fabric padded cubicle walls, the organization will occasionally take you to an off-site event in a tourist-friendly location. This largesse will depend on factors such as the economy, the company's financial performance, and whether the boss is having an internal affair with someone who will accompany him. While off-sites are a superficial attempt to boost employee morale and build camaraderie, they are also a quagmire of potential minefields and you need to stay alert at every step.

The Journey

Capitalizing on group fare discounts, employees usually travel together. If there's a bus or train ride involved, you can be dead certain that a feckless game of antakshari will take place soon into the journey. An enthusiastic Madonna will pipe up, 'Chalo, let's play antakshari,' and others will pitch in with 'Good idea!', 'Bhalo,' or 'Saras che'. Teams will quickly be formed, men versus women or the left side of the bus versus the right side, and the aforesaid diva will start singing. Half the orchestra will join in, a quarter will clap politely and the remainder will pretend to sleep. Let's be clear—despite your self-confidence, you have absolutely no singing skills, so restrain your vocal cords and simply try to look like you're having fun as 'song beginning with mm' and 'song beginning with pa' reverberates through the bus. Raise your hands and sway when the typical 'Yamma yamma, yamma yamma' noise starts for 'song beginning with ya'.

Rooming arrangements

Irrespective of your designation, a true sense of your organizational aukaat (worth) comes from the rooming arrangements. Your room is one of the best indicators of your position within the corporate hierarchy.

Separate hotel: While everyone typically stays together, sometimes enough rooms aren't available and some employees are shunted to an alternate hotel. If you are one of them, start sending out your CV even as you are being transported out. You're completely irrelevant and were probably invited to the off-site by mistake.

Sharing rooms: If you are made to share a room with a colleague, shame on you. If you aren't deemed worthy enough for your own shower and bed, the organization has little faith in you and it will manifest in time to come. An overhaul of the CV is highly recommended.

Single room: Thankfully, you are at the equilibrium of the rooming see-saw and you can, in complete privacy, breathe a sigh of relief. But be cognizant that you have colleagues sleeping ahead of you, in the next two categories.

Upgrade subject to availability: Hotels frequently offer a few complimentary room upgrades to large groups which are then distributed to a select few participants. If your boss decides to enhance your room, it's only a matter of time before he does the same for your responsibilities. You have been marked out as a high potential resource so have a good night's rest, knowing that you are sleepwalking on the road to success.

Guaranteed upgrade: The standard protocol for hotels is to offer one guaranteed room upgrade; the most influential suit gets the suite. If it's you, you have arrived, you Jacuzzi-soaking, bathrobe robing czar.

Conference Rooms

Irrespective of how exotic the locale is, most of the time you'll be yawning in the conference room, so get familiar with its important aspects.

Seating

Choosing the right seat is the most crucial decision you'll make as the objective is to make eye contact with as few people as possible. Boardroom seating is the worst as you have to look at virtually everyone on the table. In this scenario, take either of the seats at the extreme end as everyone will be to one side thereby halving the number of people you have to stare at gloomily. Round tables are somewhat better since you only have a couple of douchebags on your table to interact with. Theatre style or classroom seating is ideal to get lost. Don't sit in the front rows where you will need to feign attention. Don't stay in the back rows either as seniors will keep stepping out to take calls and then lurk at the rear. Take a seat in the middle of one of the centre rows; there's nothing like the middle-middle to while away time without anyone noticing.

Temperature

Trace the shortest route to the restrooms because conference room thermostats are permanently set to 16 degrees and coupled with all that bottled water, you will need frequent nature breaks. Also, dress in layers because you'll invariably be compelled to offer your jacket to that hot colleague who always feels cold.

Goodies

Meetings customarily have treats ranging from bowls of saunf (fennel seeds) to assorted confectionery on the table. Have your arm reach the bowl immediately as you sit down because you never know the replenishment schedule that the staff follows. These are also excellent opportunities to restock your personal stationery and swipe all the complimentary writing pads, pens and pencils—the kids at home will appreciate it.

Team-Building Activities

Teamwork is an inexplicable yet unavoidable part of corporate life. As the cliché goes, 'There is no I in TEAMWORK,' but unfortunately, there is 'WORK' which is completely needless.

This instinct to make a barren of mules do doltish tasks in a controlled environment is enhanced during off-sites. HR usually organizes activities such as building bridges using newspapers, walking tightropes blindfolded or playing outdoor games. These team-building actions are utterly useless and don't hold your breath on getting anything out of them. The only thing they motivate you to do is to actively consider quitting your job. Twenty-four hours and everyone's back to the usual office politics, only bonding over discussions about how asinine the management is.

Stay in the background and do the bare minimum required to demonstrate participation. Don't give opinions, creative inputs or try to drive consensus—water will find its own level and decisions taken in the same manner as they are back in the office. There will be jostling and bickering but finally the senior will lose patience and autocratically state what's to be done. Blindly follow.

Strategy Breakouts

Equally worrisome is the leadership's proclivity to have participants break out into groups to discuss a topic of apparent importance and then present their analyses. This is a no upside-downside only situation and your sole objective should be to form the perfect group, comprising the following:

| The enthusiast | He is passionate about the company, leadership, breakout topic and just about everything. He's been active throughout the off-site and will lead the way in hard work; make sure he is on board. |

The calligrapher	Whether you are using white boards, chart paper or post-its, someone will need to keep notes. Get a person with good cursive handwriting as it will save the entire group a lot of effort.
Your twin	While a good team supposedly has members with complementary skills, ensure that at least one person has the same expertise as you. When required, he can step in to do the work rather than you having to.
The water boy	Get someone who is even more disinterested in the proceedings than you are. He will unfailingly keep strolling out to the lobby to grab snacks and can get back refreshments for the posse—nourishment is very important.
The vocal cynic	Have someone who is perpetually aggrieved at everything. He will draw all the negative attention, thereby leaving you under the radar.
The bouncer	Invariably the group will break down in dissonance and matters will grind to a halt. Recruit a bouncer with authority to step in and get matters back on track.
The buffoon	Set up a buffoon to ask silly questions, make inane suggestions and draw raised eyebrows from the rest of the clique. If others look bad, you automatically look good.

The patsy	Theoretically, all of you are working together; practically, identify the weakest link on the team who all can point fingers at when things blow up. Discuss internally and the only consensus you need to drive is who the patsy will be.

Assemble this cast of characters and let the enthusiast and cynic fight it out while the twin does your work and the calligrapher takes notes. The bouncer will step in with white flags and the water boy with masala peanuts. When it comes to presenting, the buffoon will draw the flak and when the fat lady sings, the patsy will get the blame. Lots of ideas will be discussed, forgotten and discarded, just like the chart papers pasted around the conference room.

The Gala Night

Every off-site ends with a grand celebration where the leadership shows up in ill-fitting casuals and the rest in the only set of now crushed party clothes that they had packed. The middle managers get busy introducing their team to the seniors, who are circulating around the room like waiters. The DJ is setting up his console. The emcee is practising the pronunciations of all the important surnames. And the jacket lenders have initiated their efforts of trying to hook up with their respective jacket lendees.

Drinks management

Off-sites are relaxing places to down a few—the seniors are in a good mood, colleagues are looking surprisingly hot, there is no office the next day and the spouse is far away minding the kids. But that's when things go downhill and every event invariably ends with someone getting supremely drunk, getting into a fight and becoming the talking point for weeks to come. You need to avoid being him.

Abstaining is the best way but equally, you don't want to spend all night un-coolly shaking your head at, 'Just have one small drink, dude.' So, take a drink and nurse it while you place mental bets on which colleague is going to make his career-limiting move. Alternatively, order mocktails like vodka-tonic or Rum-cola without the alcohol. Wonder why plants around function areas are more lopsided than usual? Because smart professionals like you surreptitiously pour their whiskies in them. 'Are you ready for another one,' the boss puts his arm around your shoulder. 'Sir, yes, Sir!' you exclaim and soon enough, the bougainvillea is rewarded with another peg.

Food management

Your gastronomic behaviours equally influence your corporate perception. Come across as a sophisticated professional and grab a mini meal in your room before the party. While your colleagues are wolfing down their grub, you can just keep up appearances and skilfully manoeuvre the food around your plate. Post dinner, while others belch and burp, intelligently sip green tea and discuss the economy.

Formal sit-down dinners with fancy crockery and cutlery, custom name-cards and menus, etc., are stressful. When given fixed menus, choose only one item from each course— one soup, one appetizer, one main course, one dessert. 'Get me everything, I will try it all,' is not appropriate. Don't snap fingers or whistle to get the butler's attention; ring a little bell or clap your palms elegantly. One's never sure about the correct positioning of the water glass or which spoon and fork to use for what course. Break someone else's dinner roll and you effectively ruin the pattern and force everyone to go in the wrong direction. Can you imagine the repercussions—'We want Rishi to lead this critical project? The imbecile led the entire table astray at dinner yesterday.' So just wait until someone makes the first move and quietly follow.

In buffet settings, the strategy changes but the overarching principle is still to appear distinguished. While others grab a plate and dive in, sampling each dish, start with a systematic reconnaissance of the buffet. Step back to the outer perimeter and circle in a concentric pattern. Don't commit yourself too quickly but walk around mentally recording all options. Then select and stick to one cuisine; don't mix the paneer makhani with Hakka noodles or pita with pasta—it is inelegant. Avoid messy foods that require excessive force to cut, bite or eat—no curries which can splash, bones that can fly, beans that make you gassy, chillies that make you belch or noodles that hang from your lips. Salads, thick soups, dry vegetables and seedless fruit—your food choices should be exactly like what you hope your career to be—benign and non-controversial.

The awards ceremony

Sometimes, employees are given an additional boost of motivation through an awards ceremony. Whatever. If you receive an award, stride up on stage smartly, don't wave or hoot and don't mention your parents in your acceptance speech—no one cares. Thank your bosses for their belief, your colleagues for their support and dedicate the recognition to your wonderful team. Place your palm on your heart in gratitude and exit stage right.

If you are the top dog on the dais handing out prizes, get the rhythm right—shake hands, give the award, guide the winner to a spot next to you, have a photo clicked and then guide him off. Some winners will inadvertently disrupt this routine but like the good shepherd, keep your flock on track. Keep in mind that you are being videotaped and photographed through the event so look engaged at all times.

Dancing

For the finale, the DJ will spin tracks on a makeshift dance floor and the room will split into three groups, basis designation and dancing awkwardness. The early careers will burn the floor, jiving and twerking in perfect rhythm to the music. The senior leaders will be at a safe distance, leaning against the bar, tapping their uncoordinated feet and awkwardly bobbing their heads to the beat. And the self-conscious middle managers will clumsily sway at the edge of the boogie zone. Their moment in the spotlight will come every few songs when an early career will pump his hand up and down like a locomotive driver and people will line up behind him, holding each other's waist. An office train will form and wind its way around the floor and this is when the mid-managers will jump in with raspy *Chug Chug* sounds. And when the train derails they will hurriedly scurry away, like sound sensitive roaches airdropped at a David Guetta concert.

Occasionally, a flock of early careers will rush to the bar and drag a senior leader to the dance floor. 'One dance only, Saar!' they will exhort and he will have no choice but to go with them. All pairs will break up and form a circle around the leader who is now forced to dance in the centre. For a few minutes, the entire crowd will watch aghast as he makes his moves and phones will be out, taking videos and selfies. Not wanting to risk being the protagonist of the net's next viral video, the leader will sidle out at the next lull between songs.

Group Photographs

All events have a mandatory group photograph with all participants gathered in front of a photographer who tries to get the widest-angle shot possible. The typical formation for this photo is as follows:

- The CEO seated in the centre, flanked by his senior executives and as many ladies as can be accommodated
- A row of enthusiastic early careers kneeling in front of the seated people
- A row of short mid-managers standing behind the seated people
- A row of tall mid-managers standing behind the short mid-managers
- One breakaway senior leader standing with the mid-managers, ostensibly sending a message that he is one with the troops

THE GROUP PHOTO

For years to come, the senior leaders will scrutinize the photograph as they evaluate their weight gain and check out their office crushes. With the objective of getting some face time whenever they check the snap, place yourself as close to the senior executives row as possible. You can even try plonking on one of the chairs if no one notices. If your height is relegating you to the last row, stoop and join the shorties in the row ahead. But no matter what, don't affiliate with the front row. A kneeling mid-manager screams failure.

Early careers should kneel gracefully; the leadership should marvel at your style and poise. Do not squat, an abhorrent pose to record for posterity, irrespective of how strong your quads are. Place one knee on the ground and clasp your arms classily across the other thigh.

If all have been given custom T-shirts, monogrammed with the company's logo and slogan, wear it. This is not the time to be a fashion rebel. If you are one of those XXXL sizes, then inform the organizers well in advance; you don't want to be the only obese bumpkin in street clothes because the T-shirt doesn't fit. Resist smart-alec comments and stick to the script—the photographer will say 'Cheese' and you will go 'Cheese'. Not butter, not bread, not Nutella—just cheese.

Finally, be patient—don't make faces, grimace or check your watch in annoyance. A poor chap, who you will never see again, is balancing precariously on a chair to capture an artificial display of team spirit. It can take some time.

In Conclusion...

Offices are desolate and distressing places. There are the occasional efforts made by the organization to inject some joy into the melancholic environment, through off-sites, parties or other celebrations, so approach these carefully. If you can make it through inconspicuously, without getting involved in any significant drunkapades, you'll be just fine. Alternatively, if you have the confidence, ability or panache, be uber-cool and memorable to stand apart from the crowd. Jump into the pool fully clothed, score a century at beach cricket, dance like a rock star, beat the boss in arm wrestling, make a kick-ass presentation—be remembered. These events can speed up that next promotion or bring your career to a skidding stop. All in the backdrop of a beautiful holiday location.

FEEL GOOD ANECDOTES

Crouching tippler, hidden dragon

For those with the smug view that dipsomaniacs only crawl out of the woodwork at sales conferences and two-wheeler distributor meets, this example should burst your bubble. Copious amounts of alcohol peppered with long-standing animosity towards one's boss can bring out the drunken warrior in any of us.

The United Nations, that organization where world leaders discuss peace, poverty and other good karma stuff, held an off-site in the Austrian ski resort of Alpbach. The UN Secretary General Ban Ki-moon got together some of his top officials for a few days of introspection and some rounds on the slopes. Like most retreats, this had a gala dinner and one of the senior participants was invited to toast the leader. Up shot the tipsy hand of Mr Sha, the undersecretary general for economic and social affairs.

The top-ranking official from China at the UN had been sampling the cocktails for a while now and staggered his way to the stage. After his cordial 'Ni Hao, ladies and gentlemen,' he descended into a drunken tirade directed at arguably the world's most powerful diplomat. 'I know you never liked me, Mr Secretary General—well, I never liked you either,' he stated to the horror of all in the room. He then expressed his regret at having to leave his supply of home-made dimsums to come to the Big Apple—'I didn't want to come to New York. It was the last thing I wanted to do.' And then stated what was by now crossing everyone's mind, 'You've been trying to get rid of me. You can fire me any time, you can fire me today.' Ban Ki-moon smiled and nodded awkwardly, as he mulled how to tape his employee's mouth shut with pink slips.

UN officials present tried to convince loose cannon Sha to give up the microphone but he was having none of it. Not satisfied with pissing off his boss, he directed his ire at Bob Orr, from the executive office of the secretary-general, 'I really don't like him: he's an American and I really don't like Americans.' The entire rant lasted about ten to fifteen minutes but according to a senior official who was present, 'It felt like an hour.' Sha probably woke up the next day with a terrible hangover and kept a low profile, as his colleagues giggled at him for the rest of the retreat. No one is sure how his year-end appraisal went.

16

JONATHAN VISITING SEAGULL

*The nuances and nuisances of regional and
global visitors*

 A typical multinational corporation divides
its business into geographic regions. The
various countries in a region (e.g. Asia) report
to their respective regional office (e.g. in
Singapore/Hong Kong), which in turn reports
to a global head office (e.g. in New York/London). Therefore,
every role has at least three executives—the Global CEO,
Regional CEO and Country CEO or the Global Head of
Marketing, Regional Head of Marketing and Country Head
of Marketing and so on. As a country executive, therefore,
it's very probable that in addition to your local boss, you
will also be reporting (whether straight line/dotted line/
matrixed) to regional and global bosses. You need to
manage all of them.

Regional and global bosses are just about as useful to your
business as blood to a vegan vampire, but can't be ignored

either. They will be in your hair until they fulfil their three step Collate-Degenerate-Transfer responsibilities.

Collate

They wake up every morning and ask themselves a fundamental existential question, 'What do I want to collate today?' They are experts at designing templates, bullying markets into completing them and using cut-paste-macros to organize all that data into one consolidated report, which they pass off as their performance. For example, they will add up revenues from all countries and claim credit for delivering the grand total. They clearly don't have any direct responsibility but fervently believe that their collation skills positively influence your operations.

Degenerate

There are many ways to destroy franchises, and they have mastered all of them. They might annually update and circulate a comprehensive document called *Business Standards, Global Guidelines* or the equivalent. This 'one-size fits all' rule-book has to be adhered to by all countries within their kingdom. Or they might run an RFP (Request for Proposal) for a multi-nation deal in the hope of achieving 'economies of scale'. So one global marketing agency will win the mandate for all markets or one hardware vendor will supply computers across the world at predetermined global rates. Now the negotiated rate will typically be much higher than what countries have been paying locally, so it gets awkward for you—convincing your vendor to take more money for the same product because of the crappy deal struck by your respective Head Offices.

Transfer

Finally, they are expected to track all key initiatives across markets and share the best practices and successes with others. They merely regurgitate their learnings from place to place and one frequently hears them location-dropping, 'When I was last in the Philippines, I observed their awesome digital marketing campaign that reaches the same customer segments that you folks in India are targeting. I will connect you guys.'

They hold regular conference calls where countries dial in to give their respective updates; the regional boss then provides useless inputs with the others on mute. Or he visits, usually when the weather's good, to give aforementioned perspective in person.

Visualize a seagull that flies to an island, settles down and deposits some droppings. Then it flies away to another island and shits there before coming to home base for a while. Shortly after, it takes off again. That's what regional folks are—seagulls who go from place to place, leave some excreta and depart. In fact, let us call all of them Jonathans.

Sucking Up to The Seagulls

Impressing Jonathan isn't difficult. No one cares two hoots about him at home and giving him even a little attention during his visit will floor him.

Pamper him like a king

Start his king-of-the-world treatment from the moment he lands. He's used to taking the airport metro back home, instead have him received by a chauffeur, or better yet a mid-manager from your unit. Position it internally as an opportunity to get face time with an influential international senior and there will be riots for the coveted airport pickup duty.

An ATG (Aarti-Tikka-Garland) routine is a must at the hotel he is staying at. A hotel representative should wait in the lobby with a silver tray and lamp that she rotates in a clockwise movement around his face when he arrives. That's the aarti. She should then dip her finger in a bowl of vermillion and smear it on his forehand. Hello tikka. And finally take a wreath of flowers and put it around his neck. Welcome garland. This routine will quickly immerse Jonathan into Indian culture, as also your heart.

Jonathan loves constant attention and his coffee mug, like Lord Krishna's inexhaustible vessel, should never be empty. Mid-managers should be trained on the briefcase dive and whenever he makes a move to leave, should lunge to help him with his bags. Finally, make sure that he has uninterrupted access to two essentials—bottled water and internet connectivity, and depute a manager to continually shadow him with an icebox and mobile hotspot.

Boost his self-esteem

Indulging in activities usually reserved for celebrities will boost Jonathan's self-esteem significantly and a confident Jonathan is a happy Jonathan.

Have him inaugurate a new branch, store or the office library and unveil a plaque with his name on it. Schedule an interaction with a group of early careers and mid-managers, who have been classified as high potential employees. He will be thrilled to share perspective with the company's future leaders and they will be highly motivated at listening live to a foreign accent. Layer on an opportunity for him to hand out some autographed certificates to employees; seagulls love to preen for photographs.

Make him walk around the office, going from floor to floor, shaking hands and making small talk with small designations. Or organize a town hall with all employees. Welcome Jonathan and thank him for visiting the franchise. He will take the stage, thank you back, and then turn to the audience and ramble about how excited he is to be in this dynamic country. Sometimes his English won't be intelligible but brief the translator and ask him to cue the audience suitably. 'Jonathan has narrated a funny story. Please laugh,' or 'Jonathan has stated an interesting fact. Please say Ooooh.'

Integrate him into the culture

Ensure that Jonathan takes back some traditional local gifts for his family—if he earns brownie points at home, so will you. Organize a curated shopping trip by preselecting some shops at the local market and capping the amount that the shopkeepers are allowed to fleece him for. Have a mid-manager accompany Jonathan around, again dangling the 'quality time with a regional senior' carrot to justify their colossal waste of time.

Finally, it's on the bucket list of all visitors to India so if you can have him visit the Taj Mahal, Jonathan will be indebted for life. If not, at least put on a cultural experience for him—a Kathakali or Bharatnatyam dance, an elephant ride, a fortune-teller reading or anything else he might have seen on the '*Hymn for The Weekend*' video. Make his wildest stereotypes come true.

Presenting to The Seagulls

The more time a seagull spends with you, the more questions he'll have and the more he'll interfere in the future. Your primary objective, therefore, is to keep him occupied elsewhere. That said, Jonathan will expect one mandatory presentation and while the previously discussed presentation strategies are also applicable to regional visitors, here are some specific tactics that you can execute.

Present when jet-lagged: Schedule your presentation for as soon as he lands; he will be jet-lagged so welcome him with a strong cup of decaffeinated coffee. Then watch him doze in and out of sleep on the conference table.

Showcase mind-blowing facts about India: Start the meeting with a soulful rendition of the national anthem, a ritual that he probably hasn't experienced in other markets. Then showcase the uniqueness and scale of India with some mind-blowing attention-grabbing facts on the first slide:

- India at 1.3 billion people is the world's second largest country
- One in four Indians is between ten and twenty-four—the youngest nation in the world
- India has twenty-two major languages written in thirteen scripts and over 700 dialects—every 40 km, therefore, there is a new dialect, food, dress, customs, etc.
- 125 million Indians speak English in India—more than double the population of UK
- At any point, an estimated one million Indians are masturbating furiously

Mix up all the numbers: Muddle up your financial

performance by playing with exchange rates. Present some numbers in the local currency, some in US dollars, and some in Jonathan's home currency. Give him a malfunctioning calculator if you find him getting confused. Further bewilder him with India-specific units of measurement like lakhs and crores, which would be a first for him. Explain that one crore is one hundred lakhs and ten lakhs is one million and spell it as lakhs on some slides and lacs on others.

If you are completely baffled right now, imagine his plight. **Give summary bullets:** Finally, do not debate his ideas, far-fetched and irrelevant as they may be. Just nod at everything he says, assure him that you will implement his suggestions and then discard your notes as he boards his outbound flight. He will be too busy shitting in the next country to follow up with you. Directly give him the few summary bullet points that he can regurgitate to his boss and other markets as learnings, 'Jonathan, if there are just three things that I want you to remember from this visit, it is A, B and C.'

That's all he really wants.

The Senior Leadership Dinner

One sees this scene played out in fancy restaurants around the nation—a bunch of executives attentively listening to a lone foreign man or lady at the head of the table. They are trying hard to follow his accent, drawing cues from each other on when to laugh politely and making the same small talk. 'Is this your first trip to India?,' 'You like spicy food, eh?' etc. This is the mandatory senior leadership dinner with Jonathan which takes place during all visits. For you it's an opportunity to suck up and position yourself for the next job abroad and passing him the salt-shaker might be your career-defining moment. For him it's a painful few hours he must tolerate out of hunger and you are as relevant to him as the peon in the Chandigarh sector 13 branch is to you.

Indian food will usually upset his sensitive tummy so don't be too experimental. Skip the greasy and fried foods and stick to kebabs—grilled, mild and tasty. Avoid chutneys and pickles—just hearty helpings of protein. For soup introduce him to the concept of 'one by two'—the portions are still reasonably sized and you save a couple of bucks. But despite all your precautions, you will find that Jonathan will invariably spend more time in the bathroom rather than the boardroom. Do not stress and just slip him some antacids under the door. Diarrhoea is a badge of honour for him and he will animatedly share this experience with his colleagues back home.

Snagging A Do-Nothing Regional Job

Many professionals seek to leave the country for a plum international job. For this you need the support of the country leadership, who can export you either as a reward or as a punishment; work out which option is more likely.

For the reward route, project yourself as one of the architects of any successful initiative that was presented to Jonathan. Once he has sold the idea to another market and they get down to implementation, they will need help and who better than someone from the core team? Position yourself appropriately and you will invariably receive a call from an international area code asking you to pack your bags and help transfer the success abroad.

People are sometimes bumped out as a punishment because they are damaging the local franchise but are still not incompetent enough to be fired. It's not easy to hustle this punishment so operate perfectly on the cusp of mediocrity yet good intent. The seniors should want you out of their life but not the organization, and will push you towards a visa interview at the next available opportunity. Gratefully grab it.

In Conclusion...

Jonathan can be as harmless as a teenager's facial acne or as painful as a thrombosed haemorrhoid—it all depends on how you manage him. Indulge him, impress him and side-track him. As the mantra from an ancient scripture goes, *athithi devo bhava*, the guest is equivalent to God.

But don't get too attached. Because one day, without warning, Jonathan will get laid off. While regional jobs are extremely low stress and well paying, they are about as secure as a credit card at a Bangkok massage parlour. For every global CEO who believes that the regional office adds value, his successor declares it unnecessary bureaucracy. Regional offices go through alternate cycles of hiring and lay-offs as each CEO changes. So don't invest a lot of time in the crumbs that you feed Jonathan. He is but a seagull and he'll eventually fly away.

FEEL GOOD ANECDOTES

While the intention of Jonathans making cross-cultural success transfers is quite commendable, it would be helpful if they applied some more diligence before they did so. Here are some translation blunders made by large multinationals:

- Parker marketed a ballpoint pen in Mexico with its Spanish ads reading, 'It won't leak in your pocket and make you pregnant,' instead of 'It won't leak in your pocket and embarrass you.'
- The Coors Brewing Company translated its slogan, 'Turn it loose' into 'Suffer from diarrhoea' when they launched in Spain.
- Braniff International Airways translated its slogan tom-tomming its fancy upholstery, 'Fly in leather' into the Spanish equivalent of 'Fly naked'.
- Scandinavian vacuum manufacturer Electrolux tried to appeal to Americans with its slogan, 'Nothing sucks like an Electrolux'.
- Schweppes Tonic Water was translated to Schweppes Toilet Water for a campaign in Italy.
- A large Japanese travel agency was puzzled when it entered foreign markets and was flooded with enquiries for unusual sex tours. Not quite sure why this happened to the Kinki Nippon Tourist Company.
- General Motors was appalled to see that their Chevy Nova bombed in Mexico. Until they realized that Nova translates to 'It doesn't go' in Spanish.
- Sega paid millions to make the Italian soccer team Sampdoria a laughing stock. The big SEGA on their jerseys translates to 'masturbation' in Italian.
- American pharmaceutical manufacturers were intrigued at the stir their medical containers were causing in Great Britain. The caps simply instructed people to 'Take off top and push in bottom.'

The royal Jonathan

Prince Philip, Duke of Edinburgh, is the husband of England's longest serving monarch, Queen Elizabeth II. Over the seven decades of their marriage, he has travelled with her all over the world. Much-loved with an absolutely wicked sense of humour, here are some of his best quotes as he traversed the globe. We can only imagine the stir he would have caused if he were a corporate Jonathan rather than royalty.

'Ghastly.' – his opinion of Beijing during a tour of China

'If you stay here much longer, you will all be slitty-eyed.' – to a group of British students during a visit to China

'It looks as though it was put in by an Indian.' – his reaction on seeing a fuse box during a tour of a Scottish factory

'So who's on drugs here? … HE looks as if he's on drugs.' – to a fourteen-year-old member of a Bangladeshi youth club

'It looks like the kind of thing my daughter would bring back from her school art lessons.' – his reaction on being shown primitive Ethiopian art

'You look like you're ready for bed!' – exclaimed to the President of Nigeria who was dressed in traditional robes

'A pissometer?' – his question when he saw the piezometer water gauge demonstrated by Australian farmer Steve Filelti

'Get me a beer. I don't care what kind it is, just get me a beer!' – at a dinner in Rome hosted by Italian Prime Minister who offered the finest Italian wines

'Aren't most of you descended from pirates?' – in the Cayman Islands

'Can you tell the difference between them?' – when told by President Obama that he'd had breakfast with the leaders of the UK, China and Russia.

'It's a pleasant change to be in a country that isn't ruled by its people.' – to Alfredo Stroessner, the Paraguayan dictator

17

MCBCs

*The hated tribe of Management Consultants /
Business Consultants*

You may sometimes encounter an unfamiliar face in your boss's cabin, the hallway or even your workspace. Usually, it'll be during turbulent periods such as management changes, mergers or impending lay-offs. This mystery person could simply be a new employee finding his way around, but god forbid, could also be a management consultant or business consultant—MCBCs, as they are commonly referred to in the Indian subcontinent.

MCBCs possess no tangible skills, have no real-world experience and are a waste of high thread-count suit material. But they are sharp observers and make diligent notes which they report back to the top management. They can inflict serious harm to your career so it is critical that you quickly identify any consultant in your vicinity and adapt accordingly.

MCBC Identification Checklist

While they have the typical *Men in Black* persona, aspects of their appearance, behaviour and distinct conversational patterns give them away. Briefly engage with a suspected consultant and complete this checklist to determine whether he is one or not.

Appearance
- ☐ Designer clothes, shiny shoes, neat haircut, swanky eyeglasses and Fitbit
- ☐ Broad, cheesy smile showcasing bleached teeth

Accessories
- ☐ Branded overnighter plastered with business class and concierge tags from leading airlines and hotels
- ☐ Kick-ass presentation in a neatly bound file folder with perfectly formatted slides, awesome charts and a well-organized table of contents
- ☐ Accompanied by laptop-toting recent graduates from top B-schools

Communication
- ☐ Highly articulate
- ☐ Faux accent which is a strange mix of American, Australian and Irish
- ☐ Talks continually and speech is peppered with buzzwords and jargon
- ☐ Makes conditional statements—If A then B else C unless D in which case E
- ☐ Master at generalizations, extrapolations, passing judgments and making sweeping motherhood and apple-pie statements

Red flags should go up if you check more than half the boxes and to be doubly sure, do a final check and slap him with a 'Shut the heck up, you good for nothing MCBC.' If he stays calm and unruffled, he's obviously used to this and might even politely ask you to explain why you acted the way you did. Rest assured, he's a management consultant.

Winning the Assignment

The fact that your organization is even considering doling out money on consultants implies that it is in dire straits. And as soon as they get a whiff of a prospective kill, MCBCs from leading firms will swarm the executive floor like wildlings in the *Battle of the Bastards*. They will make credential presentations on how awesome they are at nothing, provide examples of fixing other industries that faced similar situations and refer to ground-breaking work done by their international offices. Their clients will stay anonymous ostensibly for privacy reasons but in reality, consultants don't want any linkages to the debacles that they created there. Senior consulting partners will invite your leaders to strategy conferences and whisk them abroad to get face time at strip clubs. They will form foursomes for weekend rounds of golf, the only occasion when they are above par in anything. MCBCs will do absolutely anything because in your mandate lies the college tuition for their children.

A Typical Consulting Engagement

If consultants could just remain aggravatingly useless in their own organization, it would be fine. As long as you don't have to interact with dolts, it shouldn't matter. The hitch is that they infest your organization and suck your intelligence and time with more fervour than leeches at a nudist camp. A typical consulting engagement is an exasperating ten-step process.

1 **Understanding the problem:** Once in, MCBCs will try to understand the problem they are supposed to solve. They will do this by interviewing everyone, from the security guards to the senior management, and ask numerous open-ended questions that start with a 'Tell me about, Explain, Describe, Why is'. All these require a detailed answer and after quizzing each person for hours, they will finally ask the one important question, 'What is the problem?' Not that it matters because they will ignore everyone other than the CEO—whatever he opines will be assumed to be the issue.

2 **Framing the problem:** Once they have a problem statement, they will put it in a rectangle and draw lines in all directions. They will put some other geometric symbols at the end of each line and then slap some buzzwords in each of the shapes and call them drivers. The better the framing, the prettier the problem picture.

3 **Hypothesize:** Now that they have a likely problem, they will go to a bar to brain-drizzle the solution. Forming three hypotheses on possible solutions, they will draw lots and rank them. The rest of the time on the engagement will be spent proving one of the theories as the panacea for all ills of the organization.

4 **Planning:** They will make a list of all the time wastage activities that need to be done—interviews with employees and competitors, research, field visits, excel modelling, flowcharts or rolling dice. The more analyses that they claim to do, the longer it will take and the more money they will make. Quite like the world's oldest profession, management consultants get paid by the hour to screw people.

5 **Data requests:** They now push the ball in the client's court and make solving your problem into your problem. They will ask for exhaustive data, files, reports, registers, etc., on short notice and circulate a daily tracker of what's pending. The onus is squarely on you and the more inadequate that they can make you feel about the quality of your data, the better they are doing.

6 **Interviews:** They will plant themselves in your cabin and interview you on your data. Paraphrasing your views in their words, they pretend to share new insights but as the cliché goes, they are borrowing your watch to tell you the time. Whenever they see you getting irritated, they'll draw the meeting to a close and send a follow-up meeting request on the way out.

7 **Replicate:** Around now, MCBCs will start replicating exponentially. This week there are two consultants in the office, next week four, and the week after eight. Very soon, you can't distinguish between employees and consultants. It's like watching amoeba from another planet, regenerating before your very eyes.

8 **Analysis:** Whenever they are not drinking coffee, they will pretend to do some analysis. They will read notes, conduct research, ask their partners for opinions and narrow down on which of the three hypotheses makes the most sense. Once done, they will schedule a meeting with the CEO and on the basis of whatever he thinks the solution is, rework the data to validate that.

9 **Prewiring:** As they near the end of the assignment, they will get the project sponsors and anyone critical to settling their bills in sync with whatever they have done. They'll run them through their key slides and make sure it's aligned with what they were expecting. If not, they'll make changes accordingly.

10 **The presentation:** The last step is scamming all constituents through a kick-ass presentation. The challenge is that they need to convey to the audience whatever the audience already knows. But that's what MCBCs excel at—they will take your data but just make it so rehashed and appealing that it appears as something brand new. They will support it with some theoretical notions and abstract statistics and somehow integrate everything for the sole purpose of solving the problems of your organization. The leadership team will gape in amazement. While you debate whether you should leap out of the building or not.

In Conclusion...

Do not be fooled by their suaveness—management consultants are as worthless as the P in psycho and it is no wonder that they are so hated. That said, consulting can be an excellent career path for readers with degrees in uselessology and the determination to achieve nothing at work. Consulting firms have honed their recruiting processes to unearth and groom such talent. So, if you have an innate knack for convincing others on how fascinating things can be, without lifting a finger, you should consider becoming an MCBC.

FEEL GOOD ANECDOTES

Shining the moonlight in la la land

So you are organizing the biggest event in entertainment with the Who's Who of Hollywood in attendance and an estimated one in eight people around the world watching live. There will be pre-parties, red carpets, post-parties, performances, and thirty-four awards to be given to the most accomplished artists. Each award will have a shortlist of nominees and the presenters will announce the winner, preselected by top secret voting, to the audience. And hopefully, all will go as per plan because you have the world's best professionals to micromanage every aspect of the event, and just to make sure that nothing goes wrong, you have PwC, a pre-eminent global accounting and consulting firm, to tabulate the votes and determine the winners. Lastly, to be entirely sure, you even get two PwC partners, each earning millions of dollars a year, to do the minimum wage job of handing over sealed envelopes, with the winner's name, to the announcers.

And such were the preparations for the 89th Academy Awards or Oscars. It was a perfectly executed ceremony and PwC partners Brian Cullinan and Martha Ruiz were standing at smart attention in the wings. As each pair of presenters entered the stage to announce an award, Cullinan and Ruiz would hand them the respective envelope with the winner's name—a smooth, much rehearsed process. However even they didn't know it at that time, but the water they had drunk before the event would soon be making a guest appearance in their underpants.

The event reached its grand finale—the award for the best picture of the year—and Mr Cullinan was to hand over the envelope listing *Moonlight* as the winner. He was, however, 'distracted'—tweeting photographs of the actors and actresses around him, and handed over the wrong envelope to presenters Warren Beatty and Faye Dunaway. They opened it and announced nominee *La La Land* as the winner. The *La La Land* crew joyfully clambered on stage and started making their acceptance speech; Cullinan was probably still taking selfies and Ruiz doing the mannequin challenge since neither rushed to correct the error. It was minutes that seemed like hours, before someone finally figured out what the heck was happening. The supposed winners, still floating on cloud number nine, were rudely cut off and it was *Moonlight*'s turn in the spotlight. They stumbled onto the stage in a daze and started delivering their acceptance speech. It was quite a ruckus, live broadcast around the world, though it probably didn't match up to the brouhaha at the next PwC partners meeting.

It really wasn't that difficult—thirty-four awards, thirty-four envelopes—just hand over the correct envelope. But trust consultants to screw it up.

THE DOOR IN
YOUR FACE

18

DUMB CHARADES

Optimizing the appraisal process

In the corporate world, you will frequently encounter people providing unsolicited feedback and as a rule, only listen to critics who agree with you. You can, however, make exceptions for people who can directly influence your career through appraisals, promotions, job changes, etc. Show them respect by demonstrating only cursory, and not utter, disdain for their opinions.

At your end, avoid giving any feedback as it's a waste of time and effort. 'All's good, couldn't be better' should be the standard reply to anyone who wants your opinion on anything. Sometimes, you may have to provide supposedly anonymous responses to 360-degree or employee satisfaction surveys and be effusive in your praise. This isn't the forum to vent out grievances and maybe HR is tracing your IP address for future retaliation. Be polite, diplomatic and promptly click submit. Any disparaging sentiments should only be shared via unsigned, fingerprint dusted letters sent directly to a regulator.

Appraisal Discussions

The mother of all feedback sessions is the annual performance appraisal. Positioned as an employee development initiative, it is simply an attempt to mess with your mind by condensing a full year's work into a quick discussion of your shortcomings and a single digit rating.

The most effective counter for someone jerking your chain is to tighten it around your fist and punch the living daylights out of him. An effective framework to do this during appraisals comes from the field of medicine and psychiatry—the 'change curve'. This was developed basis the ground-breaking research of Elisabeth Kubler-Ross who exhaustively studied people when they underwent periods of high stress. She interviewed hundreds of terminally ill people and classified their varying emotions into the following five stages of grief.

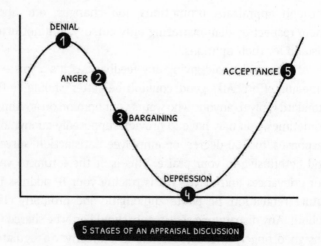

5 STAGES OF AN APPRAISAL DISCUSSION

Stage	Description	Kubler-Ross Example
1. Denial	Refusal to accept that you are going to die	'It cannot be.'
2. Anger	Resentment and frustration that you have contracted this medical condition while others haven't	'Why me?'
3. Bargaining	Desperately searching for any remedies	'Please God, I will be a better person if you make this alright.'
4. Depression	Disappointment and withdrawal into a shell	Silence and tears
5. Acceptance	Reconciliation to the situation and for whatever is to happen	'I accept whatever life has to offer.'

While one can't compare a deservedly poor performance assessment to contracting a terminal illness, use the adapted *Job Be Damned* appraisal curve for your discussions. Once the boss has completed his spiel and communicated your rating and bonus, go through the five stages of grief:

1 **Denial:** Stare at him wordlessly in amazement, with wide eyes and open mouth, until he squirms uncomfortably. Then break the silence with a loud scream,

'Are you out of your freaking mind, you lard!' Express outrage at the little worth that he has for your contributions, gesticulating with your hands as you set fire to pretend barrels of midnight oil that you burnt for the organization. Completely deny that a rating this bad is even possible and blame him for letting such a basic error slip by unnoticed. 'It's all a mistake and HR must have mixed up my ratings with someone else. Those screwballs can't staple paper right and you expect them to work a spreadsheet?'

2 **Anger:** He will try to pacify you with reconciliatory words. Go berserk. Bang the table, fling items from his desk, pace around, punch the walls, slam doors and shake with intense anger—he needs to be shivering in fear now. End by spitting on the bonus letter that he just handed over to you.

3 **Bargaining:** Other than his fearful eyes occasionally darting to the speckles of phlegm glistening on the page, you have his undivided attention. Propose ways to salvage the situation. Can he correct your rating to what it should have been? How about a larger raise or an out of turn promotion instead? A few extra weeks of vacation maybe? Hear out his counter offers and bargain hard for the benefits that you deserve for his screw-up.

4 **Depression:** He is probably losing patience by now so move to depression. Let the tears flow freely, lower your tone and appeal to his sensitive side. Share sob stories of the sacrifices that you made so that he could prosper. Talk about how your aged parents were depending on your bonus for that long due surgery. Weep without constraint; if you sense his hand on your shoulder, it's a win. If his eyes are glistening, it's a glorious victory.

5 **Acceptance:** Your theatrics notwithstanding, nothing will likely change in this appraisal cycle but you have stood your ground and set the boundaries for subsequent years. He will think twice about messing with you the next time. Shake hands and walk out stoically. No sorries, thank yous or warm farewell hugs—he has screwed a year of yours and let him repent in silence. If you spat on the letter, leave it as a reminder of your indignation.

It's simple. Irrespective of how you have been rated, your immediate reaction should be to go through the appraisal curve and claim that you deserved at least a notch higher. And if you have been given the highest possible rating, drop that battle and fight the monetary war instead. Only a 300 per cent bonus? Be appalled and start gathering sputum in your throat.

Unsalvageable Appraisal Discussions

Irrespective of how bad the year has been, step up your efforts in the last few weeks before appraisal. Show up early, leave late, turn in assignments on time and copy your boss on more emails than usual. His short-term memory will recollect this vividly and he will extrapolate this temporary burst of hard work to the full year, reflecting in a better rating than deserved. However, if in your considered opinion, the year is completely down the tube, you have two options.

Confession

Quite like 'Forgive me father, I have sinned…' at church, pre-empt his fireballs and lay out everything that went wrong before he has even settled down. 'I should have worked more efficiently and finished my project on time, I could have been more courteous to my co-workers, I ended up missing a few more weeks of work than I planned ...' Once you have already detailed your goof-ups, there is little he can add. Like a priest doesn't pummel a contrite sinner, your boss will decide to focus on the few strengths that you have and the rest of the conversation will be about leveraging those for the good of the organization. By the end, he will be so upbeat about your potential that your confession will be long forgotten and the rating not as bad as deserved.

Negative assertion

Alternatively, throw caution to the winds and cheerfully welcome all his assaults with negative assertion, essentially agreeing to whatever he says.

> Boss: 'Rishi, you are not a team player.'
> You: 'Yes, I admit I do work better alone.'

> Boss: 'Rishi, you are stupid.'
> You: 'Well, I never claimed to be the most intelligent person around here.'

Negative assertion puts bosses on the back foot because their preparation for this meeting has gone to naught. Take it a step further by adding on some negative enquiry and eliciting extra criticism, which befuddles them even more.

> Boss: 'Rishi, you are not a team player.'

You: 'Yes, I admit I work better alone, but what makes you say that?'

Boss: 'Rishi, you are stupid.'

You: 'Well, I never claimed to be the most intelligent person around here. But can you share some examples where I did things differently from how Einstein might have?'

Confession gives some hope of escaping with a mediocre rating but bruised ego. Negative assertion is a sure shot spot at the bottom of the bell curve but with pride intact. Your decision depends on how much family wealth you have backing you.

Finally, every bad rating has a silver lining and hereon, flatly refuse to accept any additional work. Every time your boss tries to palm off some project to you, retort sarcastically, 'Ooh, important work. Why don't you get it done by your star employee whom you rated Outstanding? He will do it so much better, won't he?'

An island in the sea of incompetence

Sometimes, the boss will start comparing you to peers, so never get sucked into the honey trap of learning from others on how you could have done things better. As soon as you see him going down that route, humbly yet firmly state, 'Sir, I request you to not compare me to anyone living.' This will usually be met by silence as he processes your request and as he starts to clear his throat, reiterate, 'I don't compare myself to anyone living. No one ever has.' That pretty much kills that chain of conversation right there.

In Conclusion...

No one really likes the whole goal setting and performance appraisal process. Your boss doesn't like it—it's not easy to give feedback. You hate it—it's not easy to have someone point out, however right they may be, how useless you are. But it needs to be done and get through this exercise as best as you can. And always remember that when it comes to goal setting, understate your potential. When it comes to appraisals, overstate your achievements. It's that simple.

 FEEL GOOD ANECDOTES

You may be insecure at your knack for snatching defeat from the jaws of victory. Hopefully, some of these real-life screw-ups will give you the comfort that your allergy to success is perfectly okay.

That won't even cover the credit card bills...

Imagine that a young mother tells her little boy, 'Score well on your exam, Johnny, and I'll have a chocolate cake waiting when you're back from school.' An excited Johnny skips to his classroom, his mouth watering. But as he is writing the paper, a tornado sweeps across his neighbourhood and razes their house to the ground. His mama, lucky to be alive, crawls out of the rubble and weeps as she inspects the damage to the kitchen.

But mother nature cannot destroy another mother's nature. Johnny's mama gets into her SUV and drives into town, swerving around fallen trees and corpses, to the village bakery to get Johnny a cake. There's just one slice of sponge cake left and she grabs that and races back. Alas, the road is wet and her tires old and the vehicle swerves and crashes down an embankment, flipping as it goes down. She emerges from the wreckage and weeps for the second time that day, but in her hand she holds a battered but edible piece of cake. Bleeding profusely, she crawls the eight miles back home, just as the school bus pulls in and Johnny rushes down the steps. He stops in horror as he peruses his wrecked house and tattered mama, 'Mama, I wrote my exam well. Where's my cake?' he whispers. She cries for the third time that day and with love, gives him the slice of cake.

What do you think Johnny should do? If, has read this chapter he should fling it on her aching forehead and storm out of the house. That's effectively what an Executive Vice President at AIG did when he received his bonus in March 2009. But let me step back.

AIG was one of the world's largest insurance companies—ranking six on the Forbes Global 2000 list in 2007 and dozens of executives were raking in the moolah. But there was a global financial meltdown in 2008 with AIG being one of the central players. It was on the verge of a spectacular bankruptcy until the US government intervened with a $170 billion bailout, more than the GDP of 150 countries. While many employees left or were sacked, some were requested to stay back with promises of a retention bonus, including this EVP. And so he did, even working '10-12-14 hours a day' but the situation continued to worsen and shortly before the retention payouts were to be made, AIG declared a loss of $99 billion for 2008.

Having declared the most massive loss ever suffered by any company in the history of companies, AIG must have reneged a bit on the bonus expectations they had set. But the employees accepted it, right? After all, they had taken the world to the brink of financial doom and used hard earned tax dollars of American citizens to bail them out. Not really. Our AIG Johnny was so livid when he received his bonus that he charged into the office of the CEO and gave him a piece of his mind. Well, not just that. He wrote a whiny stinker to the CEO and published it in the *New York Times*. He accused him of bending to the government and the riff-raff common Americans and declared his intent to leave AIG as soon as possible. And so pissapointed was he at his measly bonus that he magnanimously proclaimed that he would donate every piddly cent to charity.

We can't entirely blame him as AIG did stoop pretty low to screw him over, paying him a measly post-tax bonus of $742,000 (~Rs 5 crores).

It happens once in a blue moon

Imagine that you have just one master tape of a really important event—your wedding, your child's first birthday or that porno home video. I'm sure you'll be pissed—your spouse probably more so—if you accidentally delete or overwrite on it. Well, NASA, which is responsible for the US space program, mistakenly erased the original recordings of the first moon landing. So you know the original footage of

Neil Armstrong bouncing in his space suit and Buzz rushing to catch up—it's gone!

Apparently, in an effort to save a couple of bucks from their $20 billion annual budget (roughly double of what India spends on education each year), NASA took 200,000 tapes and magnetically erased them to reuse them. And the moon landing happened to be in that batch. Luckily, someone had a copy which NASA used to digitally master and replicate but the bona fide moon landing video, folks, and this may fuel conspiracy theorists even more, is gone forever.

The fat and the furious

Ever experienced the pain of booking something online and hitting the 'Buy' button a tad early, just to watch in horror as your credit card gets debited for something that you didn't really want? Now multiply that pain 27 billion yen times.

A trader working for Mizohu securities wanted to sell one share of newly listed J-Com, a company that recruits staff for the telecom industry, for 600,000 Yen. He entered the trade and left to do whatever traders do in their free time.

Unfortunately, as he and the rest of the Tokyo Stock Exchange were to discover, he had punched in a trade to sell 600,000 shares for 1 yen each. Considering that J-Com had only 14,000 total shares outstanding, the ownership of the company changed fifty times over the next few hours thanks to this trade. The price plummeted faster than one could say Sushi-san and by the time the big bosses at Mizohu discovered what was happening, they were over $200 million in the red. It's unclear as to what happened to the fat-fingered trader who conceivably wiped out the entire bonus pool for the Mizohu group for the next few decades. But given his lack of technological skills, it's quite unlikely that even J-Com could help him find a job.

Windows 95 ... per cent accurate

When Microsoft released their Windows 95 operating system, they programmed the 'select your time zone' feature onto a cool world map—any country that the user selected would get highlighted in a different colour. So, for example, if one hovered over India, it would light up, which was awesome. The only error was that they programmed a measly eight of the 800,000 pixels incorrectly—the disputed Pakistan Occupied Kashmir sliver in the map got highlighted when someone hovered over Pakistan and not India.

Sure enough, the sound of a billion incredulous '*Yeh kya bakvas hai*?' overshadowed the cheers from the handful of neighbours next door who even knew what a computer was and the software was promptly threatened with a ban in India. With the likely possibility of Windows getting thrown out the door, Gates likely rapped some cartographer in Redmond hard on his knuckles. The 'highlighting countries in a pixilated world map' feature was dropped altogether from subsequent versions of their software.

The precursor to making marijuana legal

In the 80s and 90s, even as the US was getting involved in military matters around the world, it was waging a 'War on Drugs' within its own borders. Children and youth of all ages were falling victim to illicit drugs and there was a concerted effort to control the menace. Creating awareness was critical and from national advertising campaigns to grassroots activities in schools, students were being reached with the message that drugs are not cool.

As part of this initiative, the Bureau for At-Risk Youth handed out awesome pencils to hordes of schoolkids inscribed with the motivational message 'TOO COOL TO DO DRUGS'. Great idea—all kids use pencils and what better instrument to be reminded that drugs are not trippy. Unfortunately, whoever designed the pencils had obviously never used one because he or she didn't seem to understand the concept of sharpening. As the pencil points broke, kids pulled out their sharpeners, shoved the pencils in and whirled away. And as the pencils got shorter and shorter, so did the motivational message. 'TOO COOL TO DO DRUGS' got sharpened down to 'COOL TO DO DRUGS.' Then 'TO DO DRUGS' and next, the simple and direct 'DO DRUGS'.

The irony is that this gross faux pas was spotted not by the bureau officials, teachers or parents, but ten-year-old Kodi, who was obviously going through fourth grade cranking pencils rather than paying attention. The horrified authorities immediately recalled all pencils, sharpened or unsharpened, and proceeded to investigate what the pencil designer had been smoking.

19

GETTING CANDID ABOUT GETTING CANNED

Converting pink slips to green bucks

More often than not, employees, especially *Job Be Damned* readers, will find themselves in times where the organization has had it with their shenanigans. Getting fired seems to be an imminent possibility and all need to be prepared.

Getting Canned

Losing a job, along with divorce, death, moving houses and illness, ranks in the top five stressful events that people can go through. Just like a gun recoils when a bullet is fired, so does society when you are. I could introduce you to a lot of friends who have been laid off but they are unfortunately still in hiding. Sure, you will eventually bounce back and find a new job but the thumb rule is that it takes a month of search for every million rupees in compensation you were making. So at a salary of Rs 2 million per annum, you'll find your next role within two months, and if Rs 15 million, get ready to twiddle your thumbs for over a year.

It's not like you will be taken by surprise; there will be numerous hints to indicate that a pink slip is on the way. Contrary to logic, you find work being reassigned rather than dumped on you. You are excluded from meetings and not marked on emails. Your spending limits are cut and the boss, who you have invested years in sucking up to, is either micromanaging or avoiding you entirely. Projects have ridiculously impossible targets and deadlines and you are being set up for failure. What is most alarming is that the management has started documenting every goof-up in what seems like a casual email but is actually an evil ploy to build a paper trail to support your impending sacking. You suddenly find yourself very dispensable.

So if you find yourself heading towards sackdom, instead of popping anti-stress pills, influence matters so that you get a significant settlement out of it.

Getting Retrenched

If you are sacked, you get nothing but a cardboard carton for your belongings. If you resign, there's the added benefit of an exit interview but nothing more. If you get retrenched however, that is you are asked to leave for no reason other than organizational or environmental factors, it could be as meaningful as winning the airport lotteries while transiting through the Middle East. Retrenchments are usually accompanied by an attractive package including special payouts, vesting of equity, support with finding a new job and so on. These exercises usually take place during times of cost-cutting or mergers when organizations lay off large parts of their workforce. But organizations could be open to let go of useless talent at all times, so getting on the retrenchment list can be highly beneficial.

Make your boss the target of your conniving ploys; the key is to be as exasperating as you can but without crossing the fine line between being an ass and gross insubordination. If he gives you any task, ask him whether it is in line with the company's mission and refuse it by stating, 'I don't think it is worthwhile to spend my time on something that is not even in sync with what the company wants to do.' If he doesn't budge, have your to-do list handy and ask him what task you should drop instead so you can work on this one.

Another way to get his goat is to try and get him sacked instead. Go to your boss's boss and complain vociferously about all the screw-ups that your immediate supervisor is making. Be outspoken and claim that you are doing this only for the good of the organization. Rope in your other staunch enemy, the HR manager, and snitch about him as well. Try and get both idiots fired and document everything on email. If they are building a paper trail to get rid of you, use your nuclear boomerang to obliterate them.

Now it's unlikely that you will succeed but you have just made it much harder for them to fire you. From being a documented dolt, you have been elevated to a bothersome pain; the repercussions of letting you go could be enormous. You will likely get called into the room to negotiate so go in with your head held high and come out with a big settlement check in your hands.

Your Transition Out

Sometimes we voluntarily seek even more dullness than what we have and decide to change jobs. While all jobs are pretty much the same when it comes to jading and burning out, there is one big upside of switching roles—transitioning. We have already explored how you can maximize the transitioning in period when you start a new job. Even more fantastic are the few months once you have resigned but are serving out your notice period—the transitioning out period.

Try not to be overly smug as you announce your resignation to colleagues and the congratulatory messages start coming in; wait until you are formally out of the company before you rub it in. People will reach out, hoping for opportunities in your new organization; start having casual coffees with anyone you might want to poach. Expectations will be rock bottom with everyone assuming that you have tuned out and any work you do is a bonus for the organization. No one is asking you to be generous so relax and take your time—don't rush on anything and simply ignore whatever you don't want to do.

Focus instead on other priorities and administrative formalities. Take printouts of files that you want to pilfer for your new role. Your boss may want a handover note so write some drivel—no one is ever going to refer to it. Prepare your farewell email, start practising your goodbye speech and don't leave anyone important out from either. Leave work early, come in late, but every once in a while announce to everyone that despite your impending departure, you are on the ball. You will feel good about yourself.

The faster you have a successor identified to take over from you, the more you will enjoy your transitioning out period; the new guy will come with boundless enthusiasm to start executing. Ensure that your boss quickly gets the faith that your job will continue to lie in equally incompetent hands once you're gone. If he has no one in mind to replace you, spend some time identifying a guinea pig—either internally or externally. Gift a copy of *Job Be Damned* to your successor; he will thank you.

When switching jobs, the last few months in your current job and the first few in the new one comprise the transition period. These are incredibly relaxing and stress-free phases and the average employee can make as many as ten to fifteen transitions in the course of a career. At six months a transition, this is essentially six-seven years where one can get away by doing nothing in a comfortable low-expectations environment. Maximize it.

In Conclusion...

As the late Steve Jobs once said, 'I didn't see it then, but it turned out that getting fired from Apple was the best thing that could have ever happened to me. The heaviness of being successful was replaced by the lightness of being a beginner again...' Unless you have the leadership qualities, talent and stock options that Steve Jobs had, you can ignore this quote; this is completely irrelevant for you. Getting fired from anywhere will be a real pain in the backside; getting laid off with a substantial package, however, will not. So, work towards it. Over time you may even find that it is more lucrative to keep getting retrenched from multiple organizations than determinedly working your way up one.

FEEL GOOD ANECDOTES

Most of us would love to type out our resignation letter, march into our boss's cabin and fling it on his comb-over. But while we don't have the pluck, here are some everyday folk who resigned in memorable fashion.

A career down the chute

It was another day at New York's JFK airport and a JetBlue flight from Pittsburgh had landed. Steven Slater was the flight attendant in charge and as the plane taxied to its gate, he noticed an impatient passenger standing up to grab her bags before the seat belt signs were off. Ever the conscientious monitor, Steven politely asked her to remain seated and ever the conscientious New Yorker, she asked him to eff off. And there exploded two decades of pent-up frustration of serving tea and coffee to unappreciative passengers in a pressurized cabin.

Steaming Steven took to the public address system and let loose a volley of expletives to the woman, other passengers and all of mankind. And with a 'That's it, I'm done' he activated the emergency chute, threw down his bags, grabbed a few beers from the galley and slid down. He then ran to his jeep parked in the nearby employee lot and drove himself home. The shell-shocked passengers thanked their lucky stars that Steven hadn't resigned mid-air.

A rapper on the knuckles

Marina, a twenty-five-year-old writer at a Taiwanese animation firm, was fed up with unacceptable problems such as her boss evaluating her performance and her office not having enough restaurants in the vicinity for lunch. So rather than the standard letter or email, she decided to send her boss a resignation dance video. She set up her cameras, went to the office at 4.30 a.m. when no one was around, and shimmied her way around the office to Kanye West's number, '*Gone*'. Her cribs about her miserable work conditions appeared as subtitles of the since viral video that ended with her walking out of the office with a 'I'm gone'.

When asked what he thought about Marina, her boss lamented that he wished she had shown as much creativity in her job as she did when she was resigning. Not that the company missed having a self-entitled kid on their payrolls but they came back with a creative response of their own. They uploaded their own video addressing her concerns and ended with a 'We're hiring!'

(You can view the resignation video and the company's response by searching for 'Marina Shifrin resignation video'.)

Joining the 'Band'wagon

Joey was your average room service attendant at the Renaissance Hotel in Providence, Rhode Island, delivering late night treats to semi-clad guests for little pay and measly tips. Fed up with his job and his dittus of a boss, he decided to resign with a bit of help from a full-on brass marching band. He snuck himself his band buddies into the hotel via the employee entrance and hid in a corridor waiting for his boss. As the surprised supervisor came around, Joey handed over his resignation and his chums proceeded to create the most glorious racket that they could manage. Joey walked out of the hotel, hands raised in triumph and a broad smile on his face and the band followed him out, creating an annoying din for the exasperated, now almost deaf manager. Certainly one of the noisiest ways for an employee to make an exit.

(You can view the video, keeping the volume on high, by searching for 'Joey DeFrancesco Quits'.)

The resignation that wasn't

It is always a good idea to hold onto your career switching horses until you have an offer letter firmly in hand.

Robert Kelly was the CEO of Bank of New York Mellon (BNY Mellon), one of the country's top ten banks at that time. While the world was getting swept up in the global financial crisis of 2008 (the same one which dunked our AIG buddy below the poverty line), he mostly managed to keep his bank out of trouble. He even advised regulators on financial reform and soon enough, was courted for the country's largest banking job—CEO of the behemoth Bank of America (BofA).

Kelly was supremely interested and all the public angst at the compensation of the evil bankers notwithstanding, hammered out a sweet deal. He negotiated a buyout of all his existing stocks and awards (around $25 million), an additional $25-30 million in annual compensation, and a shift of the bank's headquarters from Charlotte to New York, so that he could continue living in his palatial Manhattan town house without having to deal with movers and packers.

Confident that his discussions would fructify, Kelly let his board know what he was up to and they started their search for a successor. BofA was broadly in alignment and one fine Tuesday, Kelly announced to his board at breakfast that, 'Bank of America wants me for the job,' and that he planned to take it. They had found an outstanding internal candidate and asked him to submit his resignation and kept a press release ready for the following Monday evening.

That Monday morning President Obama called the country's top bankers including Kelly and amongst other things, admonished them on executive compensations. The cash registers in Kelly's head started jingling sirens and he could foresee his proposed outsized BofA compensation being just a fond wish rather than reality. He practically raced back from Washington to New York where the board was all set to announce his departure and begged for his job—'I want to stay,' he pleaded.

In two minds the board allowed him to keep his job so as to not create more uncertainty than quick-gun Kelly had already caused. But the damage was done and he had lost the trust and good wishes of the board, his peers and much of the organization. Within two years he was asked to leave because of 'differences in approaches to managing the company'. And this time there was no coming back.

I'll huff and I'll puff and I'll blow your Housing down

Rahul Yadav, an engineer in his early twenties, founded Indian real estate start-up, Housing.com, with eleven other campus buddies. Eager to throw money behind immature entrepreneurs who didn't know the ABC of Aao Business

Chalayein, marquee private equity and VC investors pumped in funds into the venture. Eager to reciprocate by fulfilling their fantasy of being peed over, CEO Yadav gave them golden showers to remember. He threatened a leading investor in his firm that, 'If you don't stop messing around with me ... I will vacate the best of your firm.' He then blew up millions of their dollars in a useless advertising blitzkrieg and accused a leading media group of maligning him. And one fine day, fed up of being accountable to people who had given him a measly few hundred million dollars, he resigned politely, with the following email.

Dear board members and investors,

I don't think you guys are intellectually capable enough to have any sensible discussion anymore. This is something which I not just believe but can prove on your faces also!

I had calculated long back (by taking avg life expectancy minus avg sleeping hrs) that I only have ~3L (hours) in my life. ~3L hrs are certainly not much to waste with you guys!

Hence resigning from the position of Directorship, Chairmanship and the CEO position of the company. I'm available for the next 7 days to help in the transition. Won't give more time after that. So please be efficient in this duration.

Cheers,
Rahul

The board convinced him to withdraw his resignation. But in what seems to be an emerging trend, boards are discovering that the best way to deal with nuts is to display their own. And they sacked him a few months later.

20

CONCLUSION

As you have hopefully found, *Job Be Damned* looks at the corporate world through a lens of real-world practicality. Rejecting much of the flapdoodle of conventional management books, it expounds pragmatic wisdom that actually works. If you diligently follow the strategies outlined here, you can be sure of a long and uneventful career in the organization that you have chosen to pretend to work for. And all this knowledge can be condensed into ten simple secrets.

Secret #1: Stay under the radar

Traditional wisdom suggests that one must be proactive, show initiative and seize opportunities to differentiate oneself from the crowd. However, your net salary credit will remain pretty much the same, whether you are proactive, reactive or inactive. Instead, stay under the radar and bide your time for as long as you can; don't stand out but

225

don't disappear either. Try to be a part of everything but accountable for nothing. Be nothing more than a pinging blip that makes an occasional appearance to remind the radar operator that it exists.

Secret #2: Align with whoever is ahead

The corporate engine is fuelled by power struggles with one eventual winner amongst many losers. Internally, have no affiliations but to maintain external pretences, align with whoever is ahead and be the first to embrace the winner. Send a congratulatory message, wear a big smile and walk up to shake his hand. Sure, the sherbet may taste like urine, but ask for a second glass.

As the old saying goes, be careful whose toes you step on the way up because you never know whose ass you will have to kiss on the way down. Align with your bosses who control your life; with regional visitors who can bail you out abroad; and with high potential juniors who you may eventually report to someday. The key to long-term advancement is to never be a threat to anyone. Don't sulk, always look positive, have no permanent views or positions on anything and you will eventually float your way to the top.

Secret #3: Set correct expectations from the start

You have a long career to get through, set the right expectations early on. You are not going to part oceans, walk on water or build an ark to save anyone. You will just come into work and hopefully decompose peacefully in your cubicle, so don't give false hopes about how fantastic you are. Always follow the simple rule of under promising and over delivering. Talk down whatever you plan to do to rock bottom levels and then achieve what any average person might have done.

Secret #4: Information is power

In an organization, he who has the information, dominates. The CEO gets his power not from his Superman undies but from the fact that he has access to more intelligence than anyone else. He knows what the board is plotting, what the upcoming financial results look like and even what banned websites you were surfing at work. That is authority.

Concentrate on collecting information, stay alert and file nuggets of data as your eyes and ears gather them. Get marked on as many emails as possible, infiltrate distribution lists and have spies around the organization. Lastly, guard information as zealously as a mother orangutan would her baby. Withhold all your knowledge as that's the best form of job security. If no one can take over your job, no one ever will.

Secret #5: Over manage perceptions

From the way you talk, walk, dress and stress, people will watch and judge you. Shape their perceptions by pretending to do everything right. Surround yourself with mediocrity so that you automatically look great. Ignore usual work but go the extra mile when it counts. Whether it is smearing cake on behalf of your boss or healing like Jesus using your CSR powers, live the part.

The office may be burning but let your colleagues firefight while you fiddle externally. Track competition, travel aimlessly, rack up frequent flier miles and meet new people. Focus on networking, not working.

Secret #6: Effective communication is key

Spin fantasies like they do T-shirts in Asian sweatshops and relate them in the most believable manner possible. From your first job interview to your farewell speech, this is what you will be most involved in. Ensure that you always have buzzwords handy. Whether verbal, electronic, presentations or anything else, all communication should revolve around keeping your audience significantly enthused and sufficiently confused. Your colleagues will invest in personal growth. You stay focused on effective communication—that's the best self-development of all.

Secret #7: Teamwork is for dummies

Pundits advocate a cooperative approach where all parties collaborate and split the pie in a mutually beneficial manner. Meh. Life is a harsh zero sum game—if one wins, another must lose. Cooperation is for diplomats; the central business district is a jungle and you are a lion on the hunt. The only thing you should synergize is whisky with soda post work. Focus on manipulating your team, bosses and organization so your statecraft should put politicians to shame. Teamwork is highly overrated and the only way to make a team effective is to let everyone do his or her own thing. Aim for the nirvana of TEAMWORK—to make THEM WORK.

Secret #8: Begin with the excuse in mind

No matter what tasks you take on, however simple, chances are that you will fail. Anticipate whatever can go wrong and have your CYA excuses ready before you start any project. It is essential to have a game plan to bail yourself out of the cauldron of hot water that you will frequently find yourself in.

Smart professionals do not expend energy in strategizing on what's to be done but instead question why it should be done, and not arriving at an answer, drop it altogether. If nothing gets done, nothing can go wrong and they therefore make fewer mistakes than their more proactive colleagues. Work is for vegetables and as soon as any of it comes in your direction, delegate it downwards to your juniors, palm it off sideways to your colleagues or send it back up to your boss.

Secret #9: Seek to muddle and maintain opacity

Whenever things are getting too stable for comfort, stir the pot. The opaquer you keep matters, the more effective you will be, particularly since as the creator of the opacity, only you can make sense of it. Be a snake in the corporate cesspool, wriggling in and out of situations with minimal fuss. Throw people off, blow some covers, shock and awe— whatever it takes to divert attention.

Secret #10: Have a short-term view of everything

Finally, forget the long-term perspective and focus on the clear and present now. Stay concerned with the month's performance, quarter's share price and year's appraisal. Any seed that takes years to bear fruit is not worth planting, and in any event, be a lumberjack not a gardener. Other professionals will be there to deal with the effects of your reactive and myopic decisions. Appreciate that your job is transient and do not get too attached to it.

Creativity is hard to nurture. Leadership can be extremely demanding. Integrity is almost impossible to sustain. Risk taking is highly stressful. Collaboration can be tiresome.

So don't even bother attempting to exhibit any such lofty qualities at the workplace—you will be lonelier than a Tinder user with a rotary dial phone.

Instead, focus your attention on the strategies shared in this book, which most of your colleagues and bosses are already well versed with. If you are a senior leader, you have probably already implemented much of this in the past. You now have an impetus to develop new patterns to keep your troops sufficiently off balance. If you are a mid-manager, you are assumedly honing your career management skills and you will find *Job Be Damned* to be an invaluable guide; quickly make course corrections and catch up with the rest of the chumps clambering up the ladder. And if you are an early career, you have now been given as strong a foundation as one could possibly need. Pull up your socks and get ready to embark on a satisfyingly banal journey to a stunningly mediocre career.

THE JOB BE DAMNED SURVEY
Crystallize your career path

This unique survey analyzes four variables—your industry, organization, boss, and work, to determine whether you should be hanging on or damning your job. Follow the instructions in each section and while keeping your fingers crossed, tabulate the results.

Your Industry (A Horse or a Donkey?)

Please select only ONE of the options in each question below:

1. In the last budget speech, the finance minister said
    _____ about your industry:
    A. Something positive
    B. Nothing
    C. Something negative

2. Your industry provides a goods or service that:
    A. People fundamentally need, e.g., condoms
    B. Is good to have but can be done without, e.g., pizza
    C. People would be better off without, e.g., management
        consulting

3. Your industry's growth rate last year:
    A. Was higher than the country's GDP growth rate
    B. Was around the country's GDP growth rate
    C. Was lower than the country's GDP rate

4. Your industry's products are:
    A. Exclusive and high value
    B. Regular good quality stuff
    C. Commoditized junk

5. You can count the number of strong competitors on the:
    A. Fingers on one hand
    B. Fingers on two hands
    C. Fingers on lots of hands

6. The industry in the past year:
   A. Has introduced game changing new products/ technologies/processes
   B. Is doing some investment in R&D but nothing specific has materialized
   C. Has done nothing differently

7. How difficult is it for a complete newcomer to start in this industry?
   A. It will be impossible for someone to start afresh
   B. Extremely difficult but possible
   C. No barriers to entry; anyone can join the party

8. The risk of the industry becoming uncompetitive or obsolete due to online trends or other factors is:
   A. Impossible
   B. Could happen but unlikely
   C. Definitely could happen

Instructions

Count the number of As that you have ticked: _____
Count the number of Cs that you have ticked: _____
Calculate A – C (subtract the # of Cs from the # of As): _____

If the number above is positive, put an 'H' for Horse in the box below. If it's zero or a negative number, put a 'D' for Donkey in the box below.


```
┌─────────────────┐
│                 │
│                 │
│                 │
└─────────────────┘
```

Horse Industry: A Horse industry has strong foundations and yet is well adapted for change. Such industries produce goods or services that add value to clients, have strong barriers to entry that limit new competition and exhibit steady year-on-year growth.

Donkey Industry: A Donkey industry is one which is well poised for decline, if it isn't braying down that path already. Its products are almost irrelevant, growth is non-existent, innovation has stagnated and competition is extremely fragmented.

Your Organization (Energized or Asleep?)

Please select only ONE of the options in each question below.

1. Financially, your company:
   A. Makes a profit
   B. Breaks even
   C. Makes a loss

2. Your company is:
   A. Investing and growing
   B. Stagnating
   C. Cost-cutting and shrinking

3. Your company is ranked:
   A. In the top 10 per cent within the industry
   B. In the top half
   C. In the bottom half

4. When it comes to customers, you have:
   A. More happy customers than unhappy ones
   B. More unhappy customers than happy ones
   C. Not many customers

5. In the past year, your organization has:
   A. Merged with or acquired another company
   B. Hired people from competition
   C. Lost people to competition

6. Your company has a brand that:
   A. Most people are aware of and recall
   B. Some people are aware of and recall
   C. Has no brand

7. The orientation of your company is:
   A. Global—thinks big even if it doesn't have any processes or customers abroad
   B. National— limited to the country
   C. Frog in the well—limited to the state or city

8. The culture of your company is:
   A. Entrepreneurial
   B. Changes every time the CEO does
   C. Bureaucratic

9. Given complete freedom of choice, you:
   A. Would buy your company's products and services
   B. Don't use these products or services anyway
   C. Would buy a competitor's products and services

10. The technology and systems in the organization are:
    A. State of the art
    B. Could be a bit more up to date but they are serving the purpose reasonably well
    C. Well, we do have some calculators that we all get to share

Instructions

Count the number of As that you have ticked: _____
Count the number of Cs that you have ticked: _____
Calculate A – C (subtract the # of Cs from the # of As): _____

If the number above is positive, put an 'E' for Energized in the box below. If it's zero or a negative number, put an 'A' for Asleep in the box below.

```
┌─────────────────────┐
│                     │
│                     │
│                     │
└─────────────────────┘
```

Energized Organization: An Energized organization is ahead of the pack and focused on building and maintaining its ranking and leadership position. It is investing in growth, its brand, and is sharply customer focused. It boasts strong financials, competent management and a dedicated workforce. It is efficient in its working and entrepreneurial in its mindset.

Asleep Organization: An organization that has taken matters for granted can be considered as Asleep. Growth, if at all, is anaemic, customers are ignored, management is sluggish and its vision is myopic. Adequate investments are not being made into technology, brand, research or people.

Your boss (Moron or Rock Star?)

Please tick ALL the statements that apply to your boss. There is no limit on the number of statements that you can select.

My boss...

1. Makes things up when he is not sure
2. Takes credit for my work
3. Loses his head in times of crisis
4. Blames the team when things go wrong
5. Doesn't invite me to meetings even though I have done the work
6. Doesn't take employee appraisals seriously
7. Doesn't foster teamwork
8. Doesn't pay the bill when we go out
9. Abuses people
10. Hides information
11. Says he cares about customers but doesn't give a damn
12. Says he cares about quality but doesn't give a damn
13. Rarely travels on work
14. Has never invited me home
15. Doesn't know my spouse's name
16. Believes he is always right
17. Doesn't have any specialized expertise
18. Doesn't value my perspective
19. Never gives feedback clearly or consistently
20. Praises people only in private
21. Takes too long to decide

22. Thinks only short term
23. Works nights and weekends
24. Has a favourite on the team and I'm not it
25. Accepts wedding invitations with an 'Oh, my chance is gone!'
26. Gives the same task to many people and pits one against the other
27. His biggest contribution to a project is naming it
28. Makes impossible commitments to others and then puts the onus of execution onto me
29. Reacts impulsively to situations
30. Has been in this same job for years
31. Gets insecure if I talk to his boss
32. Will be upset if he sees me reading this book

Instructions

Count the number of ticks. If you have ticked more than seven traits, your boss sucks and put a big 'M' for Moron in the box below. If you have ticked seven or less, put an 'R' for Rock Star.

```

┌──────────────┐
│              │
│              │
│              │
└──────────────┘

```

Moron Boss: A Moron boss is insecure, uncommunicative, political and an absolute dolt to work for. He cares only about his personal growth and posturing within the organization rather than the good of the customers, team or individuals.

Rock Star Boss: She is an inspirational, secure and communicative leader. She cares about you as a professional as well as individual and knows that in your success lies hers. She is an effective decision maker, delegates efficiently and steps in when required to iron out issues. She is liberal with her praise and balanced in her criticism.

Your Work (Orgasmic or Nightmare?)

Please select only ONE of the options in each question below.

1. I spend _____ on my daily commute to work:
   A. Less than 60 minutes
   B. 60 to 90 minutes
   C. More than 90 minutes

2. To achieve optimal work–life balance in my present job, I need to add some more:
   A. Work
   B. It's already balanced
   C. Life

3. When it comes to my colleagues:
   A. They are better than my friends
   B. I don't really interact much with them
   C. With colleagues like these, I don't need enemies

4. Despite my misguided sense of self-worth, I believe that:
   A. I get paid more than I deserve
   B. My compensation is just right
   C. I get paid less than I deserve

5. In terms of recognition:
   A. I get awards and recognition regularly
   B. I stay under the radar other than an occasional compliment from my boss
   C. I never win anything

6. People in my office are:
   A. Hot
   B. It's an irrelevant question
   C. I haven't noticed

7. I work in a:
   A. Cabin
   B. Cubicle
   C. Workstation or open area

8. The goal setting process is:
   A. Goal setting is crystal clear and I know what is expected of me
   B. Never clear, so appraisals are vague
   C. We don't have an appraisal system

9. I last attended a training and development programme:
   A. Within the past year
   B. Within the past two years
   C. What is training and development?

10. My job:
    A. Makes a difference in the lives of others
    B. Makes a difference to no one other than myself
    C. Makes a difference to no one including myself

11. I last updated my CV:
    A. More than six months ago
    B. A few months ago
    C. Within the last few weeks

12. From my office computer, I have online access to:
    A. Anything I want—social media, online shopping, etc.
    B. Only sites that are relevant to my job
    C. Nothing other than the intranet, if at all

13. I get approvals from seniors or other departments through:
    A. Email with minimal follow-ups
    B. Telephone with follow-ups required
    C. Face to face with follow-ups required

14. When it comes to vacations:
    A. I manage to take all my leave for the year
    B. I carry forward whatever I don't use but end up using it eventually
    C. I end up having to lapse a lot of my leave

15. My job:
    A. Helps me develop some specific skill or expertise that will hold me in good stead in the future
    B. Adds nothing to my CV but doesn't hurt it either
    C. I am doing the same monotonous thing daily and will eventually make myself obsolete

Instructions

Count the number of As that you have ticked: _____

Count the number of Cs that you have ticked: _____
Calculate A – C (subtract the # of Cs from the # of As): _____

If the number above is positive, put an 'O' for Orgasmic in the box below. If it's zero or a negative number, put an 'N' for Nightmare in the box below.

Orgasmic Work: This is as good as a job can get. Your deliverables are clear, you have the resources you need, you are developing skills and you have adequate work–life balance. You enjoy collaborating with your colleagues and the freedom in your job.

Nightmare Work: Your job is a terrifying ordeal. You don't really know what you are doing and neither does anyone else. You have terrible colleagues, are getting paid peanuts, have no work–life balance, are drowning in bureaucracy and your job is adding no value to anyone, including yourself.

Final Evaluation

Reproduce the four ratings you have derived above into the individual columns below and then combine them into a composite four-letter Job Be Damned (JBD) rating and enter that in the final column.

INDUSTRY (H/D)	ORGANISATION (E/A)	BOSS (M/R)	WORK (O/N)	OVERALL JBD RATING
Example: D	E	M	O	DEMO

Basis your overall JBD rating, locate the appropriate action plan in the grid below and go ahead and implement it immediately.

OVERALL JBD RATING	SUGGESTED ACTION PLAN
HERO	Congratulations! Everything about your career is rocking. Just implement whatever you have read in this book and your life couldn't be more perfect. **STAY**
HERN	Your work sucks but everything else is great so switch roles within the organization. **STAY**
DERN	Your work sucks as does the industry. But you do have an awesome boss in an awesome organization. Suck up to your boss and try to switch roles, while still staying in his team. In the long run though try to transfer your skills elsewhere because the industry doesn't seem to be going anywhere. **START LOOKING**

OVERALL JBD RATING	SUGGESTED ACTION PLAN
DERO	Everything is rocking besides the industry—it's fine and have fun while the party lasts. Let the seniors worry about what will happen when the crash comes—you just tag along with them. **STAY**
HARO	Things are almost perfect besides the organization that you are working for. It doesn't matter—hang around till your rocking boss moves to a rocking company and takes you along. **STAY**
HARN	You are in a good industry and your boss is a rock star. But your organization is a mess and your job an even bigger one. Encourage your boss to switch jobs quickly—in his progress, lies yours. If he doesn't seem to be moving out anytime soon, you should be anyway. **START LOOKING**
HAMO	A terrible boss in a pathetic organization; much as you may enjoy your work, this is not sustainable. Start networking and move to a competitor pronto. **SCOOT**
HEMO	You have a rocking role in a rocking organization in a rocking industry. Sure, your boss has descended directly from hell but hey, he is not permanent. Continue with what you are doing and wait for him to get transferred or fired. **STAY**

OVERALL JBD RATING	SUGGESTED ACTION PLAN
DEMO	You have a rocking role in a rocking organization. Sure your boss sucks but well, it's temporary. Continue with what you are doing and wait for him to get transferred or fired. The industry sucks as well and you should start tweaking that CV—if your boss doesn't leave soon, you should. **START LOOKING**
DEMN	The bad news is that you have a crappy role and boss. The good news is that your company is great. But the terrible news is that your industry also sucks. There are too many disastrous balls in the air and you really need to get out soon. **SCOOT**
HEMN	You have a crappy role and boss. The good news is that the company rocks and the industry does too. You need to switch roles as soon as possible, preferably to another department under a new boss. If not, you probably need to start looking out as your day-to-day professional life seems bleak. **START LOOKING.**
DARO	You have a rocking job and awesome boss—unfortunately, the company and environment are far from satisfactory but what the heck—enjoy the good times while they last. But start planning to scoot in the medium term. **START LOOKING**

OVERALL JBD RATING	SUGGESTED ACTION PLAN
DAMO	You have an evil boss in a terrible organization in a pathetic industry. You love your role but irrespective, too many things are going against you and you need to get out of there fast. Find a better company, preferably in a better industry. **SCOOT**
DARN	You are in a terrible organization in a pathetic industry with a nightmare role. Sure, your boss makes Mother Teresa look like an evil nun but hanging onto his coattails can only take you that far. Get out of there fast—find a better company, preferably in a better industry. Take your awesome boss along if you can. **SCOOT**
HAMN	A good industry but crappy role, boss and company. I trust you have career websites open as we speak. **SCOOT**
DAMN	You have the blessings of Satan. Don't spend a minute more on this book and go and type your resignation letter. NOW! **SCOOT**

BIBLIOGRAPHY

The vagaries of corporate life have been extensively covered by management gurus, academicians, journalists, bloggers, humorists and of course the ultimate satirist, Scott Adams, the creator of Dilbert. It has therefore been challenging to give a new spin to such weathered topics and themes. I relied primarily on nearly two decades of experience observing these shenanigans up close and personal. This was supplemented by online research on some of the ideas and anecdotes, and I have listed the most notable sources. I am also certain that readers would have even more nonsensical workplace experiences and please feel free to share your anecdotes, feedback or thoughts at rishi@damned.com.

HOW TO PEDDLE HOPE

- Montgomery, Ben, 'TV Chef Spiced Up His Past Exploits', *St. Petersburg Times*, 17 February 2008

- Getlen, Larry, 'White House Chef Lied about Job, Degree, Knighthood and Purple Heart', *New York Post*, 6 December 2015
- http://www.news.com.au/entertainment/tv/radio/hamish-and-andy-prank-melbourne-man-and-find-out-hes-a-total-legend/news-story/c6dd8cf4c36a8fcbc0408bcf3df24611

METEROLOGICAL GUIDE TO BOSS MANAGEMENT

- Kelly, Keith J., 'Muzzle for Mad Dog – Condé Nast will Pay Seven Figures to Settle Assault Suit', *New York Post*, 22 September 1999
- Blodget, Henry, 'Managing One Million Animals Gives Me A Headache', *Business Insider*, 19 January 2012
- Cruz, Gilbert, 'Top 10 Worst Bosses', *Time*, 18 October 2010
- http://www.cracked.com/article/89_the-6-most-horrific-bosses-all-time/
- https://www.ranker.com/list/top-horrible-bosses-ever/robert-wabash

MEETINGS: AN ACCEPTABLE ALTERNATIVE TO WORK

- https://medium.com/conquering-corporate-america/10-more-tricks-to-appear-smart-in-meetings-f262c7735847

PROCRASTINATION: THE ART OF DOING NOTHING

- https://thoughtcatalog.com/g00/tamara-jenkins/2014/01/10-easy-ways-to-look-busy-at-work/?i10c.encReferrer=aHR0cHM6Ly93d3cuZ29vZ2xlLmNvLLmluLw%3D%3D&i10c.ua=1&i10c.dv=14

CYA: COVER YOUR ASS

- Murray, Rheana, 'How Lululemon Got It Wrong', *NY Daily News*, 10 December 2013

TO CC: OR NOT TO BCC:

- http://gawker.com/5994974/the-most-deranged-sorority-girl-email-you-will-ever-read

THE POWER OF MAKING POINTS

- https://www.telegraph.co.uk/news/uknews/6160159/George-W-Bush-comment-tops-poll-of-puzzling-pronouncements.html

MANAGING INTERNAL PERCEPTIONS

- https://www.thedailybeast.com/the-spy-who-tricked-hitler-the-story-of-double-agent-juan-pujol-and-d-day
- http://mentalfloss.com/article/58468/most-amazing-lie-history

MUDDYING WATERS

- http://edition.cnn.com/2001/BUSINESS/07/16/czech.morris/index.html

INSIGHTS INTO OFFSITES

- Piparaiya, Rishi, 'Out-of-Sight Offsite', *Hindu Business Line*, 25 April 2015
- Piparaiya, Rishi, 'How Do You Breakfast', *Hindu Business Line*, 14 February 2014
- Foster, Peter, 'China's UN Diplomat in Drunken Rant Against Americans', *The Telegraph*, 9 September 2010

JONATHAN VISITING SEAGULL

- https://www.linkedin.com/pulse/20141011224311-99993053-top-63-international-marketing-mistakes-pitfalls
- https://www.telegraph.co.uk/news/2017/05/04/48-prince-philips-greatest-gaffes-funny-moments/
- Oppenheim, Maya, 'Prince Philip to stand down from public life: 95 gaffes in 95 years', *The Independent*, 4 May 2017

MCBCs

- http://extratv.com/2017/02/28/oscar-controversy-heres-what-led-to-cringeworthy-oscars-mishap/

DUMB CHARADES

- 'Dear A.I.G., I quit!', *New York Times*, 24 March 2009
- https://www.reuters.com/article/us-nasa-tapes/moon-landing-tapes-got-erased-nasa-admits-idUSTRE56F5MK20090716
- McCurry, Justin, 'Too Fat, Too Fast: The £1.6bn Finger', *The Guardian*, 9 December 2005
- Haines, Lester, 'How Microsoft Offended Millions of Indians', *The Register*, 1 June 2001
- 'Slogan Causes Pencil Recall', *New York Times*, 12 December 1998

GETTING CANDID ABOUT GETTING CANNED

- http://www.dailymail.co.uk/news/article-1301798/JetBlue-flight-attendant-Steven-Slater-quits-job-style-luggage-row-passenger.html
- Benner, Katie, Tully, Shawn, 'Robert Kelly: Inside the Fall of a Superstar Banker', *Fortune*, 21 November 2011

ACKNOWLEDGEMENTS

It is only reasonable that I start by acknowledging all my bosses who demonstrated remarkable ability in managing such a supremely talented employee. Gert and Kamran, who kicked off my career by setting the 'Rock Star Boss' bar as high as it could go. Zion, who showed me how to present stories and Rahul and Jaya, who gave me wonderful platforms to narrate them. And Ram, who derailed all aspirations for a satisfyingly uneventful career, by continually adding on responsibilities despite my vociferous protests.

To Sarvesh, to whom I owe my entire professional foundation and the best boss, mentor and guide that one could have dreamed of.

And Victor, a role model and thorough gentleman—they just don't make bankers like him anymore.

I would like to acknowledge all my incredible one-downs over the years—it has been my privilege to get the credit for all the goof-ups that you guys made. And to the various teams I have managed—I'm sorry for all the tough asks, severe reviews, taxing conference calls, nasty emails, and crazy ideas. If I could go back in time and change things, and I sincerely mean this from the bottom of my heart, I wouldn't.

To all the awesome colleagues I have worked with, it has been a pleasure collaborating with you. And to each insecure dolt who ambled across my path, my heartfelt appreciation. If you had spent even a fraction of the time doing some productive work as you did scheming and politicking, much of this book would have never taken shape.

Thanks to the entire HarperCollins team and my editor Shreya, whose enthusiasm took this from a nearly shelved book to a nearby bookshelf.

Goo, Jags, Manish, Nikhil and Shroffy—if I were to appraise my friendships on a bell curve, you all would be guzzling beer on the far left. Am putting you chaps on a performance improvement plan (PIP).

For my father—a stalwart who lived his life, the world be damned style. I wish you were here to question me, yet again, on when I will start writing more serious stuff. And my mother—I hope someday corporations will have as much faith in their people and products as you do in your home remedies.

To Namita—your partnership, support and relentless push for improvement make my writing and me better.

Finally my dear Reina, Rayan and Gia—may you grow up to find your true calling so that you may never have to read this book.